THE MODERN MARCUS
STOIC MEDITATIONS FOR THE 21ST CENTURY

JASON BALL

Copyright © 2019 by Jason Ball

All rights reserved.

No part of this book may be reproduced in any form or by any electronic or mechanical means, including information storage and retrieval systems, without written permission from the author, except for the use of brief quotations in a book review.

Cover design by Deanne Longmore.
Original cover image by Mitchell Griest.
Published by Considered Content – hello@consideredcontent.com

For Kathryn and Rowan who put up with my many less-than-Stoic moments.

CONTENTS

WELCOME TO CRAZY — 7

PUTTING MARCUS TO WORK ON THE BIG ISSUES
1. Five Core Themes — 19
2. You Are Going To Die — 21
3. Live In The Now — 27
4. Too Much Stuff — 33
5. The Surprising Power Of Indifference — 39
6. Zero Degrees Of Separation — 47

THE MEDITATIONS
7. The Second Book — 57
8. The Third Book — 65
9. The Fourth Book — 73
10. The Fifth Book — 87
11. The Sixth Book — 101
12. The Seventh Book — 117
13. The Eighth Book — 135
14. The Ninth Book — 155
15. The Tenth Book — 171
16. The Eleventh Book — 187
17. The Twelfth Book — 203
18. And Now The Credits (Otherwise Known As The First Book) — 217

INDEX OF MAIN THEMES — 227

WELCOME TO CRAZY (YOU'RE NOT ALONE)

The world today can seem like an insane place. People do strange things, harbour odd motivations, make irrational choices. We get caught up in the stuff of life, seemingly oblivious to the fact that this same stuff is making our lives worse, not better. We act as if we will live forever despite all the evidence to the contrary.

More often than not, we live for any time apart from the one we find ourselves in. We live for the future – when we'll be rich or successful or famous or meet the person of our dreams. Or we live in the past – if only we hadn't done that thing, if only we'd taken more chances, if only we'd come up with that devastating comeback to that kid who made fun of us at school.

This contrasts with a 'live for the moment, dance like no one is watching' vibe that, while attractive, is something most people struggle (and fail) to achieve. And when they do achieve it, they tend to focus on trying to maximise surface-level happiness. But this is often at the expense of a longer-term, more sustainable understanding of how to lead a good life.

Of course, we think of these things as particularly modern. It's obvious that we're more status-driven than ever. We 'like' our 'friends' having the time of their lives on Facebook and Instagram. We refresh our social feeds a million times a day to combat the fear of missing out (FOMO). We follow Insta-celebrities and their carefully crafted anything-but-spur-of-the-moment posts. You know, the one about that thing that just happened that was so totally awesome.

But the truth is, these things are not so new. In fact, they would be completely recognisable to people throughout the ages. While our ancestors may not have had social media and smartphones, they almost certainly had all the ambitions and anxieties we have today (often with a more visceral appreciation that life can be brutally short).

Fortunately, some of them had the wisdom to find a way out. They were able to take a step back, to park the emotional attachment to the bigger, better, more, more, more. They were able to find a path to inner peace, self-reliance and genuine compassion for their fellow humans. They found an antidote to everyday crazy.

One such group were those that followed the philosophy of Stoicism. This articulated an approach to life that was centred on reason, fairness, justice, compassion and self-reliance. It was, at heart, a structured approach to flourishing in the face of day-to-day life.

While, today, the term stoic (with a small s) is often used as a description for someone who buries their feelings in a Mr Spock kind of way, the reality is quite different. Core to Stoicism is a deep appreciation for our common humanity and our place in a fundamentally interconnected universe. It emphasises the good of the many over the benefits to a few and stresses our duty to help those around us. But at the same time, it also recognises that, while we can try to help, all we can ever have control over is our individual thoughts (and even that can be a challenge).

Far from a long-dead historical artefact, Stoicism is an approach that has even more relevance today, when we're all pulled this way and that by the competing demands of family, work and a life lived at the speed of the internet. It's why more people than ever are turning to this timeless wisdom to give them practical strategies for dealing with the fundamental craziness of modern life.

This pragmatic approach is key to Stoicism's appeal. Unlike some philosophies that are all about the thinking, Stoicism is fundamentally about the doing. It's no surprise then that Stoicism provides the foundations for modern effective treatments such as Cognitive Behavioural Therapy (CBT). Treatments that refuse to get hung up on all the questions of a tell-me-about-your-mother variety and focus instead on a *'How can we help fix this right now?'* approach.

But where do you start?

For many, the route in is via one of three philosophers: Seneca, Epictetus or Marcus Aurelius. Between them, these three cover the main ideas and practical applications of Stoic thought. And out of the three, it's Marcus Aurelius and his *'Meditations'* that is often the gateway drug.

Marcus wrote the *Meditations* over a number of years between 170 and 180 AD. In this time, he was engaged in a war against the Germanic tribes and, as you can imagine, probably had his fair share of trials and tribulations.

The *Meditations* is split into 12 books and would have originally been written in medieval Greek. They were essentially a set of personal notes, not intended to be read by others. In this, they show the process of Marcus getting his head around what it means to live a good life – by which he would have meant an honourable, virtuous and self-reliant one.

Importantly, the original *Meditations* must be seen in the context of being written by a Roman emperor of immense personal power, though beset on all sides by fractious politicians and an easily angered population that spanned the largest empire the world had ever known to that point.

He would have been keenly aware that job security was in no way a given (27 Roman emperors were assassinated over the lifespan of the empire).

Beyond the danger of a knife in the back, these were perilous times where pandemics were rife and would sweep across the empire, killing thousands of people every day. Despite all this, Marcus is named as the last of the five Good Emperors for ruling over an age of peace and prosperity.

We should, of course, not be fooled into thinking of Marcus as some kind of saint (regardless of the impression given by Richard Harris's portrayal in the film Gladiator). This was a man who ruled with near absolute power over an empire where atrocities such as slavery were the norm. He was fundamentally a product of his time.

But neither should we write him off as a relic of the past. His thinking is, in many ways, surprisingly modern. He is a down-to-earth pragmatist. Ultimately, he has plenty to teach all of us about living life on this crazy, beautiful planet we call home.

BRINGING MARCUS UP TO DATE
Now, if you are expecting this version of the *Meditations* to be a scholarly work of translation, you're going to be disappointed. (If you've kept your receipt, you should be able to get your money back.)

There are many worthy versions of the *Meditations* that aim to be an accurate word-for-word translation of Marcus's thoughts. The problem with these is that, all too often, they replace the Greek (or the Latin translation of the Greek) with a kind of ye olde English full of thee's and thou's. As such, they are often pretty dense reading, making you work hard for the essential wisdom to be found inside.

Maybe this is a good thing. There is a theme within Stoicism that praises hard work as a virtue to be admired. But for me, all this achieves is to make Marcus's insights less accessible to a modern reader. And this, I believe, does the world a terrible injustice.

So this book starts with a different premise: *What would Marcus write if he were writing right now?*

The Modern Marcus reimagines the *Meditations* in the world we all live in today – a world of media, technology and state-of-the-art weirdness. It takes Marcus's thoughts but reframes them in language, context and, often, content.

So, while the original has quotes from obscure Roman plays, I've replaced them with comparable ones from modern films. While the original refers to prominent Romans, I refer to famous people from our own age. And while the original is centred on a world where Rome lies at the heart of life, my version reflects a world where the heart is more likely to be technological than geographic.

In doing this, I have made some changes that a purist will hate. In the original *Meditations*, Marcus refers a number of times to the gods (though he does appear to question their existence on more than one occasion). In this edition, as a man centred on the fundamental importance of reason, I portray him as a more secular figure.

As can be expected of someone writing in the second century, Marcus gets some stuff wrong. He still lives in a world of earth, wind, fire and water. A world of vapours and humours. A world devoid of the theories of gravity, evolution and chaos. (Although he is surprisingly on the ball when it comes to the fact that everything is made of atoms that are recycled by the universe again and again.) To bring him into the 21st century, I have updated some of the science while keeping it at a layperson's level.

Marcus's Rome was a male-dominated, slave-owning semi-democracy. If he were writing today, it would be in a thankfully different context (though still more male-dominated than most of us would like). So I've dropped the idea of it being fine that people can be owned like livestock.

The final thing I've changed is the position of the first book of the original *Meditations*. While all 12 books are here in their entirety, this version starts with Book 2.

There is a suspicion that Book 1 may have been written at a later date. It reads as a kind of acknowledgements where Marcus thanks his friends and family for making him the man he is. This may be because he thought that others might read the *Meditations* after his death. So, I have moved this to the back as a kind of appendix.

However, for all these changes, it is important to note that I've done everything I can to ensure the core ideas remain true to the original. The meditations in *The Modern Marcus* are in the same order as you'll find elsewhere with the same book and chapter numbers. I have, as far as I can, stayed true to Marcus's essential philosophy and worldview (even in areas where I don't buy what he says). You may disagree with my interpretation and you are, of course, free to form your own analysis of what Marcus is saying – in fact, I view this as wholly a good thing.

Ultimately, I hope that through reading *The Modern Marcus*, you will be able to get direct access to Marcus's thinking and be able to apply it to the world you see around you today.

HOW TO READ THIS BOOK
The Modern Marcus is split into two main parts.

The first explores five core themes that can be found throughout the *Meditations*. In this section, I look to bring together Marcus's thinking on issues as diverse as how we can avoid being slaves to modern consumerism and what it means to face the prospect of our ultimate deaths. This is illustrated with excerpts from across the Meditations.

The second part contains the full twelve books of the Meditations themselves, rewritten from a thoroughly modern perspective. Each meditation is numbered in the same way as you'll find elsewhere, so if you want to get a different perspective from other sources, you'll find it easy to cross-reference the texts and take a view on whether you think I've done the thinking justice.

Of course, there may be a particular issue you're dealing with – splitting up with a loved one, losing your job, being unfriended on Facebook, etc. If so, turn to the back and you'll find an index structured by themes, allowing you to go deeper into the thinking on a particular subject.

In terms of how to actually read the book, you're free to do it any way you like. You can, obviously, work through it in sequence cover to cover (bearing in mind that the original Book 1 is now at the back). The books themselves do not have specific central themes – there isn't one on death, another on love, another on duty, etc. They are simply a broadly chronological series of Marcus's thoughts.

Alternatively, you can go the dip-in, dip-out route. Each day, open the book at random, close your eyes, drop your finger on the page and read what's there. Then apply the thinking to whatever else is on your mind that day. How can that specific meditation help you view things in a new and different light? Does it offer a new perspective on something you're going through? Does it shake you out of some limiting assumption?

Be patient with this approach. While it may seem that the meditation you pick has absolutely nothing to do with your life and the challenges you face, don't be too quick to dismiss it and select another. Give it a little time. Meditate on it.

Often, it is these more oblique, more tangential thoughts that can help us get unstuck from where we find ourselves. They open up our intuition. They re-engage our reason. They free us from locked-in thinking.

However you use this book, I hope you find Marcus's wisdom and perspective a help in your everyday life. The Stoic philosophy is, at its heart, about taking action in the real world. It has been my pleasure and privilege to get to know Marcus Aurelius better through writing this book. I find myself a wiser, calmer, more centred person whenever I spend time in his company. I hope you will too.

PUTTING MARCUS TO WORK
ON THE BIG ISSUES

FIVE CORE THEMES

> *'The universe has been around for billions of years. You are a mere speck upon a speck. You are a simple collection of atoms held together in a fleshy bag of fluid. Your perception is, at best, a bit wonky and your mind is often all over the place. Your future is, let's face it, impossible to predict.'*

As with any of us, the thoughts that fill Marcus's head often return to a number of central ideas – these echo the central foundations within Stoicism itself.

So, as you read through the *Meditations*, you'll see him cycle through a number of themes that, together, provide his personal framework for how to live a flourishing life. These ideas are scattered throughout the twelve books and probably reflected the specific problems and challenges he was facing the day he wrote them.

Of course, you and I face many of the same challenges, albeit in a more modern context. We are, after all, human – with all the frailties and biases that have characterised our species for thousands of years. But as modern humans, we tend to be less patient when it comes to getting help. In short, we want it now.

So, while many answers can be found in the individual meditations, I want to take some time to pick up on the big issues and core themes within the books that have resonated with me personally and show how they can be applied in the modern world. I'll illustrate these with specific passages from the *Meditations* in *The Modern Marcus* and talk a little about how modern Stoicism can help in a practical way. In doing so, I hope to give you some practical thinking you can use right now.

YOU ARE GOING TO DIE

> *'When you decide that whatever is happening right now is all fine and good; when you're not bothered whether you've got lots to do or not very much (as long as it's all in harmony with reason) – then you won't care whether your time left on this planet is long or short.'*

Perhaps the most common theme you'll see in the *Meditations* centres on the shortness of human life (which another Stoic heavy-hitter, Seneca, writes about extensively).

The point here is that we're all mortal. Regardless of how long we have left on the planet, we're all going to die. However it happens, the end result is a certainty.

The *Meditations* were written towards the end of Marcus's life, so his own mortality may well have been a more pressing concern than would be the case for a younger man. He died in 180 AD, aged 58. This was respectable for the time he lived in but falls short of what we might call 'a good innings'.

Regardless of whether he thought of himself as old (he refers to this a couple of times in the original) or felt the shadow of the Grim Reaper sneaking up, he was remarkably unfazed by the prospect.

If we contrast this with our modern world, we see some stark differences.

The reality is, few of us ever see anyone die. Not in real life anyway. What was a natural, everyday event in Marcus's time is now largely a medical procedure, hidden from most people's eyes.

Many would see this as a good thing. But to do so is to distance ourselves from one of the most natural events in all humanity. And that distance (and widespread ignorance of how people actually die) breeds an exaggerated fear of death.

We hide behind euphemisms (they passed away, lost their battle, kicked the bucket). We chase every new fix that may extend our lives a little longer (taking vitamins, eating 'clean', not eating at all for extended periods). We expect miracles from our doctors (and blame them when they fail to do the impossible).

In Marcus's eyes, death was nothing to be feared:

> *You should always behave like your next breath will be your last. If there is a god of some sort, you've got nothing to fear anyway. If there isn't (or they simply don't care about us mere mortals) then forget them. We've evolved to deal with all sorts of challenges, why assume this all falls apart at death? You're probably more ready to face your end than you realise.* **(Book 2, Meditation 11)**

He returns to this a couple of meditations later:

> *When you really look at it, death is about as natural as things get. You might as well fear the sun coming up. In fact, death is not just a natural event, it also helps keep the whole of nature working by recycling much-needed atoms.* **(Book 2, Meditation 12½)**

Fundamentally, Marcus saw death as just another natural event (same as birth). He dwells less on the thought of an afterlife and more on the idea that all of us are made up of atoms and that, when we die, our atoms will simply disperse to join all the other atoms in the universe around us.

But while he was fine with the idea of dying, it did lead him to emphasise that it's important to act while we can, not to hesitate or wait for the 'right' moment (which may never come). We see him caution himself repeatedly against wasting time worrying about what others may think and do when he could be getting on with making the world a better place.

> *All those books you plan to read. Those tabs you have open for later. That bucket list of experiences to try before you die (someday, maybe). Do it now while there's still time. You're a long time dead.* **(Book 3, Meditation 14)**

Let's face it, none of us knows when our time will come (or, for that matter, when those around us will breathe their last). You may have decades of good health ahead of you. You may die before you get to the start of the next chapter.

Now, of course, you could play the numbers game. You could justifiably say, 'Well my dear old grandmother lived to ninety and died doing the tango with her latest boyfriend.' And because you share some of her genes, you might see this as a reason to put off doing this or that – there will be time later (mañana, mañana...).

The reality might be quite different.

While you may prefer not to think about your death (or the deaths of your loved ones), it will not change its inevitability. Ignoring it, however, may mean you spend less time and effort cherishing others. You may say *'I love you'* less often than you could (or avoid saying *'I'm leaving you'* when you really should). You might put up with shitty jobs that suck the very life out of you. You might never say, *'Screw it, let's go to Bali.'*

In Marcus's world, the pervasive presence of death served as a reminder to live. It acted as a source of motivation for the Stoics to do the very best they could with what they had for as long as they had left. It inspired Marcus to fully engage with the world around him.

If all this talk is making you uncomfortable, it could be that you simply fear death. To a greater or lesser extent, many of us do. Here, again, the ever-pragmatic Marcus has some advice:

OK, let's park the whole philosophy thing for a minute.

You're afraid of dying, I get it. Try this for size: Think of all those old people who staved off the Reaper for longer than most but are now pushing up daisies. Are they better off than those who didn't manage 'a good innings'?

Sure, they got a few more years of work. A few more years of hanging out with tolerable people. A few more years encased in a failing body.

Maybe that's a good thing. But still, they all ended up dead just like everyone else.

When you think about the 13.8 billion years to date and the probable infinity of years to come, there's not much difference between a centenarian with a weak bladder and a baby that doesn't make it out of the hospital. **(Book 4, Meditation 50)**

Maybe this feels a little brutal. But in our over-medicated age, there is often the sense that we should try to eke out our existence for as long as we possibly can, no matter what that may mean for the quality of our lived experience. For Marcus, this would be a bad deal. He would say that we should do what we can while we can so that, when the time comes, we're ready to die with no worries of things left undone.

He would also tell us to take the long view. For Marcus, birth and death are all part of a cycle. We are made of atoms. When we die, our bodies will break down and these atoms will become part of something else. While this is not a vision of an everlasting soul and a wonderful afterlife, it does give us all a sense that we are part of something far, far bigger.

He best sums this up in Book 8:

We all die.

When I pass, my children will bury me. In time, their children will bury them or see them go up in smoke. It's always been this way.

Thousands of years of smart people, arrogant people, downright odd people – where are they now? All those geniuses, gone in a flash, some forgotten, some remembered as heroes and legends.

So think about how your wonderful, complex body will one day be broken down into its atoms and scattered. Your little life extinguished and everything that makes up your body recycled by the universe. **(Book 8, Meditation 25)**

Death is ultimately a fundamental part of life. Rather than simply look at it as the end of something, we can instead view it as a way to help us begin to live better.

MAKING IT WORK FOR YOU – FIVE KEY QUESTIONS

1. If you knew that you wouldn't live to see your next birthday, what would you do differently with the time you have left?

2. Are you prepared for death – both your own and the death of those around you? How could you be better prepared?

3. What's the least rational belief you hold about death? How can you challenge it?

4. How will you maximise the quality of your life as you age?

5. Do you understand how death actually happens? (Knowledge is power.)

LIVE IN THE NOW

> 'It's pretty obvious that nothing will better prepare you for putting all this thinking into practice than the situation you find yourself in right now.'

It's perhaps a cliché to claim that there's no time like the present. For most of us, this is generally used as a reminder to get off our backsides and do the thing we've been putting off for way too long. Asking that person out. Starting that exercise regime. Cleaning hair out of the plughole. But for Marcus and the rest of the Stoics, this had a more literal meaning. As far as they were concerned, there is no time *but* the present.

Throughout the *Meditations*, Marcus often seeks to return his focus to the here and now. He repeatedly comes back to the fact that it is pointless either worrying about the past or fretting about the future. He first hits the theme in Book 2:

> It doesn't matter whether you live for three thousand years or thirty thousand, all you really ever have is the present moment, same as everyone else.
>
> You can't lose the past, it's already gone.
>
> You can't gain the future, it's not here yet (and may never be).
>
> Ultimately, there are two truths in all this. The first is that everything from the beginning of time is just a bunch of repeating patterns – you can keep watching them go round and round, but they're all the same. The second is that no matter if you die young or old, all you ever lose is the present moment – and even this

is not really yours to own. **(Book 2, Meditation 14)**

Homo Sapiens are, as the name of our species suggests, thinking apes. While many of us hope that others (and if we're honest, ourselves too) would think a little more and go ape a little less, the reality is that we all spend a lot of time in our own heads. We have big, highly evolved brains that allow us to analyse our surroundings, learn from the past and anticipate the future.

This is a good thing – especially when you're running around the plains of prehistoric Africa trying to eat other creatures while simultaneously attempting to avoid getting eaten yourself. It means you can maximise your survival, make plans to improve your lot and avoid poking that thing that killed poor cousin Ug.

But fast forward a few millennia and we find this essential skill has some downsides.

Many wonderfully caring, empathetic, sensitive people dwell endlessly on the past. They worry about what they've done. Specifically, they fret about having done the wrong thing. They regret never taking that opportunity to go backpacking in South America. They fear they've caused offence with that thing they said that one time to that person in that shopping queue. And maybe they should have tried that stuff in bed that secretly excited them rather than keeping it strictly vanilla.

Of course, when they're not eternally replaying the past, they're fast forwarding to an imagined future. For some, this is a source of worry – will I keep my job, will I ever find love, should I see the doctor about this lump? (Although if it's the last one, the answer is: *yes*.) For others, it's a way to fantasise about a brighter tomorrow (when I win the lottery, when I get that promotion, when I tell my boss to shove it and go live on a beach in Thailand).

The problem is, as Marcus points out, neither the past nor the future really exists. The past is gone. Nothing you can do will change it. You can't go back and make things follow a different course – although apologising when you've screwed up will probably help with the after-effects.

The future hasn't pitched up yet. More importantly, the future you imagine (for good or ill) will probably be quite different than the one you get anyway. Sure, you can make plans, but there's nothing to say that those around you will play along (not to mention the wider universe). And all too often, this is simply a way to put off doing what needs to be done right now – as John Lennon wrote, *'Life is what happens to you while you're busy making other plans.'*

For Marcus, the good life is about getting on with what you need to do in the present moment. As he says in Book 9:

> *What does it really take to be fully human? Precisely what nature is demanding right now. Right. Now.*
>
> *No delay. No worrying if anyone is watching. Don't try to boil the ocean, just get started. Small steps. And understand that this is a pretty big deal in its own right.* **(Book 9, Meditation 29)**

There is a simple, powerful lesson in this approach.

Too many of us grasp for the next big thing without ever stopping to focus on what's happening right in front of our noses. We rush headlong in search of the next job without spending time to get really good at what we actually do. We lust after a bigger, better (way more expensive) house without thinking about what we can do to lead a simpler, more rewarding life right where we are. And we're quick to swipe right on the next potential lover without spending time getting to know the person we've already met (and all their fascinating imperfections).

If we heed Marcus's advice, we'll narrow our focus dramatically. We'll simply do what we need to do in the moment we find ourselves in – letting the past go and avoiding obsessing about the future.

Importantly, however, this is not simply a recipe for a never-ending series of kneejerk reactions. Our lives should still be framed by the overarching narrative of trying to live a good life and doing the right thing. We should focus on reason over reaction (and particularly overreaction).

In doing so, we can begin to have a tangible impact on the world around us. Maybe not in some heroic cure for cancer way (though that would be fantastic) but in a way that would start to allay our fears about what might happen if, when, maybe. We might find that by making small but tangible gains, we can place our problems into a more realistic perspective.

As Marcus says in Book 8:

> *Don't freak yourself out imagining the entirety of your life. Don't dwell on everything that could happen, all the troubles and pain that may come your way. Instead, take each day as it comes and ask, 'What's so unendurable here?'*
>
> *You'll discover your answer may be a bit embarrassing.*
>
> *Then remember, it's not the weight of the future or the past that's pressing down on you. It's always the present that really counts.*

When you look at it like this, problems become small things. In fact, when you refuse to let things get out of proportion, chances are, you'll cope just fine.
(Book 8, Meditation 36)

As someone prone to blowing things out of proportion, I find this both practical and comforting. My imaginary problems tend to grow and multiply as I project them into the big, scary future. Taking small steps to deal with my real problems right now, however, is something I can get my head around. In fact, if I immerse my head more fully in the present, I don't have the space to dwell on what could be.

Marcus sums this up beautifully earlier in Book 8 (as well as bringing it back to questions of mortality again):

Don't worry. Seriously, don't. Everything is bound to the laws of nature and soon enough, you'll be a distant memory.

So focus on what you've got to do right now. Split reality from fantasy. Do your best. Be good. Stick to the path of an honest, just person. Be kind. That's it.
(Book 8, Meditation 5)

Pretty simple really.

MAKING IT WORK FOR YOU – FIVE KEY QUESTIONS

1. What's your biggest regret about the past that you should simply move on from?

2. What daydreams/fantasies are preventing you doing something tangible right now?

3. What are you putting off until tomorrow (next week, next year, sometime)?

4. How can you make the world of today a better place (even if only slightly)?

5. What should you stop reading this book to go and do right now?

TOO MUCH STUFF

> *'Before today, all your attempts at discovering the good life are likely to have been unsuccessful. You haven't found it in clever thinking, money, celebrity, sex, drugs or rock and roll.'*

There is a modern perception that to be stoic is to be an unfeeling android. It is often bound up with a perceived viewpoint that goes something like: *If I'm alright, then screw everything and everyone else.* Critics point out that many of those attracted to Stoicism are wealthy, successful people – people who, these same critics claim, are hell-bent on serving their own interests at the expense the world around them.

This is simply wrong.

As Stoicism has climbed the *'Ooh, that's kinda cool'* scale in recent years, its most visible new disciples have come to light primarily because of their fame rather than their life choices. And because a philosophy of honest, rational self-reliance doesn't make for great headlines, journalists have tended to focus on those that take things to the extreme.

So we hear about the so-and-so billionaire who leads a masochistic life of everyday suffering – fasting for much of the day, walking in the snow in flip-flops, taking part in ultra-endurance sports – as one *New York Times* headline asked: *'Why Is Silicon Valley So Obsessed With the Virtue of Suffering?'*

The reality, of course, is that the vast majority of modern practising Stoics are simply everyday people, doing their best with what the universe hands them. Go to any Stoic meetup or convention and you'll be surrounded by people from all walks of life, of all ages and of every conceivable political viewpoint. In short, they're a representative microcosm of the wider public.

So where does this misconception come from?

Well, one of the core ideas in wider Stoicism is that it is important to avoid getting too attached to the things and people around you. This sees its modern expression in the film *Fight Club* when Tyler Durden claims: 'The things you own end up owning you.'

When we obsess about the stuff in our lives – particularly the quest for bigger, better, more stuff – our daily existence will inevitably be skewed to supporting our addiction. This, in turn, means we'll tend to act in ways that are expedient and self-serving rather than being true to our higher selves.

We see this all around us. People living payday-to-payday who still gorge on two weeks of blowout holiday a year. People trapped in soulless jobs to pay the mortgage on a house they cannot truly afford. People whose sense of self-worth is dependent on the number of followers they have on Instagram.

The Stoics explicitly reject this thinking. But as an intensely practical bunch, they also look to put this into action.

Seneca, one of the richest men of his time, advocated practising poverty – getting rid of all creature comforts for a period and spending time with the bare minimum. This has two aims. The first is to allow us to fully appreciate what we have (you'll miss it when it's gone). But more importantly, it also enables us to understand that the kind of stuff we place so much value on isn't really that valuable after all. We don't need the BMW. We don't need the designer jeans. We don't need the latest smartphone.

Echoing Tyler Durden, Marcus puts it like this:

> *Don't lust after stuff you don't have or you'll be a slave to your wants and desires. Instead, think about the things you already own that bring you the most joy. Imagine how much you'd want them if you didn't already own them. But be careful, don't fixate on them so much that you'd flip out if you were to lose them tomorrow.* **(Book 7, Meditation 27)**

So when we scoff at rich, famous 'Stoics' and their attempts to de-bullshit their lives, we need to consider the alternative. Isn't it better to try to stay grounded and not get hung up on the consumer treadmill rather than blowing it all on expensive cars, designer clothing and a cocaine habit? Or for the other 99% of us, isn't it better to focus on the simple joys of the present rather than sacrificing 351 days a year to drudge-work simply to get 14 days on a perfect beach?

I know what Marcus would say:

> *Think about those who've lived without limits – those that have done it all: scaled the peaks of fame, plumbed the depths of disaster, surfed the waves of chance.*
>
> *Where are they now? Smoke, dust, stories.*
>
> *The examples are legion. Drugged-out actors. Burnt-out executives. Aged rockers chasing one more fix. How pointless are the things people like these chase after.* **(Book 12, Meditation 27)**

The eagle-eyed among you will have noticed that I talked about the need to avoid becoming too attached to the things and *people* around you.

It's true that the Stoics warned that it isn't just trying to hold on to stuff that's a problem, it's trying to hold on to people too. This is, perhaps, at the root of the characterisation of Stoics as unfeeling automatons.

Caring about others is a good thing. If there was a bit more common empathy in the world, it'd be a fundamentally better place. So why should you resist the pull of your fellow humans?

We'll turn our focus to that in the next section.

MAKING IT WORK FOR YOU – FIVE KEY QUESTIONS

1. What stuff is owning you? What do you have or want that limits your freedom?

2. Could you embrace a period of voluntary poverty to reset your stuffometer?

3. What do you own that brings you real joy (but that you take for granted)?

4. How can you limit the influence of people and companies who want to sell you more stuff?

5. What stuff should you throw out, like right now?

THE SURPRISING POWER OF INDIFFERENCE

> 'Anyone can live a perfectly good life if they are indifferent to things which are fundamentally indifferent to them.'

In any relationship – love, hate, family, friends with benefits, whatever – there are at least two people in the loop. In fact, in today's hyper-connected world, there are often many, many more (though we probably need to loosen our definition of 'relationship' when we move from the physical world to the mainly virtual one).

Thing is, you are only ever one part of this equation. Everyone else will have their own minds, opinions, objectives and strange quirks of human nature. It's what makes them absolutely fascinating and totally frustrating in equal measure.

The problems come when we start to think we can control others' thoughts and behaviour. Why can't they see that our way is so infinitely better? Why do they keep doing that thing? What's wrong with these people?

This is something we see in the thinking of the earlier Stoic, Epictetus, who says that core to a good life is understanding the difference between things we have control over and things we don't. The things we have control over basically come down to our thoughts. The things we can't control are pretty much everything else (especially the people around us).

Marcus picks up on the people aspect of this in Book 4:

> *You can't change people, they'll act as they will. Expecting anything different is like expecting a cat to bark. But why worry? Soon we'll be dead and a little while later, no one will remember us anyway.* **(Book 4, Meditation 6)**

Now we might argue that reality is less binary. After all, there are things we can influence, for right or wrong, even if we cannot ultimately control them. However, the key here is that people can come unstuck when they focus too much on areas they simply cannot control.

We see this in friends who want to 'fix' their partners. Or in parents who are determined their little darling follows a particular career. Or in those same little darlings later in life who are certain they should receive a promotion (and are devastated when it passes them by).

We see this illustrated in Book 2:

> *It's kind of sad when you see people going around in circles trying to get into other people's heads. The truth is, the only head you really need to get into is your own. Once you know your own mind, you can be calm, focused and at peace with the world.* **(Book 2, Meditation 13)**

In this, the Stoics would argue that it is better to cultivate a position of indifference. From this standpoint, we simply roll with the punches, the ups and downs of life. We don't take these things personally or think the universe has it in for us. We just get on with living the best life open to us within the context we find ourselves in.

Now, it's important here to make the distinction between Stoic indifference and modern apathy. Indifference isn't simply a recipe for meh. It isn't an excuse to avoid engaging with the world and not even trying to make a difference. Rather, it's about not getting too attached to the outcome of these efforts.

Marcus picks up on the need to at least try to have a positive impact on the world around us in Book 9:

> *When you're up against something you can't control, relax. When you do act, always be honest and fair. In either case, focus on making the world a better place for others while being true to yourself.* **(Book 9, Meditation 31)**

But he also cautions against doing all this simply to attract praise or rewards, this would be to fixate on achieving a positive outcome for ourselves:

> *When you've done a good deed and someone else has benefited, shouldn't that be reward enough? Why do you need anything more? It's only idiots who are desperate for prizes and applause.* **(Book 7, Meditation 73)**

This idea of indifference goes further than simply refusing to get downhearted when people and things don't do what we want. It also extends to how we react when others upset or attack us. Put simply, if we are confident we're being true to ourselves and doing the right thing, we shouldn't take it personally.

In Book 10, for example, Marcus highlights the fact that when we get angry or depressed about others' criticisms, we are giving them too much credit – it's them, not us:

> *From the moment you get up, ask yourself, 'Does it really matter if others criticise my actions when I know they are correct?' Of course not.*

> *People who are so quick to praise you or blame you are just the same in the rest of their lives. Think about all the stuff they do, what they chase after or take from others they attack – not just with their hands but with the highest part of their selves, the part that's the source of fairness, truth, honour and justice.* **(Book 10, Meditation 13)**

Marcus argues that when you are attacked, it is simply down to the culprit making a mistake or letting their emotions get the better of them. It is certainly not something that should damage our sense of self-worth. In this, he challenges us to think about how we ourselves behave and to recognise that, on a deeper level, we're all susceptible to the same kinds of impulses:

> *When someone offends you, consider whether you have similar faults. Do you too love money, fame and pleasure too much?*
>
> *Once you realise they're only doing what they do because they are driven by these impulses, you'll be less angry. What else could they have done?*
>
> *Alternatively, if you can, help them see things another way (you'll help yourself too).* **(Book 10, Meditation 30)**

Marcus does concede, however, that we should pay attention to valid criticisms and those that come from a respected source. We should, he says, take steps to correct our behaviour if someone can show that we're wrong. But for the most part, he'd take the view that worrying about whether others like us or hate us is not worth wasting time on (see the 'life is short' theme above).

Importantly, whatever happens, he'd say that it isn't events themselves that are important but rather our opinions of them. Or as Shakespeare's Hamlet would later say, *'There is nothing either good or bad, but thinking makes it so.'* Marcus makes good use of this idea, steeling us against overinvesting in others' opinions or inflating the importance of events in our heads when the reality is something quite different.

This is an important warning for us in the 21st century, watching our newsfeeds, hyperalert for signs of either praise and recognition or attacks, slights and negative triggers. We live in a time where people seem to be more eager to take offence than ever. Where freedom of speech is valued but only if it is the right kind of speech. And where this is magnified across social media, tribal politics and university campuses.

Marcus would tell us to get over ourselves.

He would argue that no matter what someone says about you behind your back or to your face, no real harm is being done. Or at least, for you to feel harm, your mind has to cooperate with your attacker. In fact, he'd go even further and say that even if someone physically attacks you, it is still only your mind that perceives the pain and that you can minimise this by detaching as much as possible from physical sensations.

He brings all this thinking together in Book 11 with nine-and-a-bit rules for anyone who wants to avoid taking offence:

When someone pisses you off, here are some things that could help.

First, *remember that we're all part of one big human family. Strip it back further and we're all made of the same atoms (mostly oxygen, carbon, hydrogen, nitrogen, calcium and phosphorus). We're all intelligent, thinking creatures who have scraped our way to the top of the pyramid on this beautiful planet we call home.*

Second, *think about what the offending person is really like in all the roles they play in their lives. What's pressuring them to think and act the way they do? How much is it all to do with their own self-esteem?*

Third, *what if they're right? Then you have no reason to complain. And if they're wrong, they've simply made a mistake. Just as no one wants to be lied to, no one wants to do wrong either. Imagine how they'd react if they were accused* of being unfair or greedy or stupid. They'd be pretty quick to get angry.

Fourth, look, just between us, you know that you sometimes piss people off too. So really, you're no different than them. On a good day, you're on top of this but the inclination is still there, lurking in a corner of your brain. Chances are, the only thing holding you back is a worry of what others would think.

Fifth, you don't really know for sure they're doing anything wrong. You can't see into their heart. People's motives are never 20:20 (even to themselves). You need to be super clear on this before condemning someone else's behaviour.

Sixth, if you're getting impatient and frustrated by it all, remind yourself, life's short. And when you're dead, who'll really care?

Seventh, it's not what they've done that's getting to you, it's just your opinions of their actions. Ditch this and the offence will evaporate before your eyes. How do you do this? Remind yourself that their offence hasn't done any real harm to you, not to the core of who you are.

Eighth, getting so wound up about it will only really damage you and won't affect the root cause of your offence.

Ninth, last one, it's difficult for anyone to resist genuine kindness. Even when someone is trying to be a total dick, it won't work if you meet them with gentle good humour. Sure, try to correct them if you can or else jump in before they get started with a 'You know, we're both fellow humans in this crazy world. You might want to hurt me but that's not how I roll. You're just going to get all worked up for nothing.'

Be polite about it. Point out how other animals don't act like this (and they aren't as smart as your accuser). But don't be sarcastic or picky. Be genuinely nice. You're not their school teacher and needn't play to the crowd (whether *they're with you in person or hovering over the retweet button). And even if there are others around, treat the situation as if it was just the two of you there alone.*

Keep all this in mind and live up to your best self. But even though you're protecting yourself from attack, don't go sucking up to anyone, especially the person offending you. That won't help.

Remember, losing your temper is never the solution. There is more to be gained from being authentically rational and humane, from being gentle and calm. That's strength. Anger is simply weakness.

One more thing, a bonus if you like: haters gonna hate. To expect bad people never to do bad things is just foolish. It's not going to happen. In the same way, tolerating them being dicks to others while getting angry when they do it to you is simply irrational. **(Book 11, Meditation 18)**

If you take nothing else from the *Meditations*, you could do a lot worse than choosing this passage.

MAKING IT WORK FOR YOU – FIVE KEY QUESTIONS

1. What do you try to control that you simply can't?

2. Who has upset you recently? What mistake were they making?

3. Think of someone you know personally and dislike – how are you similar to them?

4. For a recent annoying experience, how did your opinions contribute to how you felt/reacted?

5. What personal criticisms have you heard that you *should* pay attention to?

ZERO DEGREES OF SEPARATION

> *'Ever since the Big Bang, things have come into being in the same way and will continue to do so until the end of time. How can you claim then that everything is getting worse? That the world is condemned to turmoil and despair forever?'*

The final theme we see throughout the *Meditations* is the central idea that everything is connected. In many ways, all the other core themes can be seen as subsets of this.

Marcus views the universe as a well-ordered whole where things happen as a series of causes and effects. While Marcus's view almost certainly had more to do with the whims of the gods than ours would, in other ways this is a very modern idea.

You've probably come across the butterfly effect. A butterfly on the other side of the planet flaps its wings. This creates a ripple effect that, eventually, contributes to a hurricane forming many thousands of miles away. Marcus and the other Stoics would be absolutely at home with this idea.

For his part, Marcus picks up this theme in Book 4:

> *Whatever occurs always follows on from what happened before. It's not just a random hodgepodge of events but an orderly sequence of cause and effect. Just as everything that already exists works as part of the whole, everything new takes its place in the great cosmic clockwork too.* **(Book 4, Meditation 45)**

Now, this view could be seen as somewhat fatalistic – stuff is going to happen to you because it's the natural end result of something that happened at the beginning of time. But in this, Marcus treads a line between the 'roll with the punches' view we've already explored and the 'do what we can right now' imperative to make the world a better place.

Again, this comes down to the fact that the present moment is all we ever have. No matter how long and complex the chain of events, what's happened up until this very second has happened.

Call it fate, luck, the gods, whatever. There is nothing you can do about it. However, while that's all history, you are now free to do what you can with the cards you're dealt. It's what you do now that matters. And because everything is connected, the consequences of your actions could be far-reaching.

The good news is that you have a fair amount of freedom in your choices. You can choose to make wise decisions that play to your best self. Or you can make poor decisions and give in to your baser instincts. It's up to you. One thing you can't do, however, is mess with the laws of nature and the wider universe.

Marcus returns to this theme early in Book 5:

> So your doctor tells you to stay hydrated and prescribes a course of antibiotics. Fair enough. Of course, flip this round and we could say nature has prescribed some disease, disfigurement or disability. The former prescription is about making you better, the latter about fulfilling your destiny.
>
> Think of it like a fine stone wall, all the blocks fitting neatly together to make something whole and solid. It's the result of a series of events fitting together just so to deliver a certain outcome.

We might say, 'So-and-so had it coming' and yes, they did. Just as we accept our doctor's prescription (even if the medicine tastes foul), we should also accept what the world serves up. It's just part of the way of things.

In fact, there are two reasons why you should chill out about what happens to you. The first is that it is the inevitable result of a whole series of events seen and unseen that was always going to end at precisely this point in time. The second is that these events are part of the universe, and to change what's happened to date is to break the whole (good luck with that).

So quit bitching about it. **(Book 5, Meditation 8)**

This inability to change the fundamental nature of the universe should appear blindingly obvious. But a quick look around provides ample evidence of people who seem to believe they can wish their version of reality into existence. Or seem hell-bent on living in a make-believe fake reality where only their actions matter. One where they're free to do what they want with no consequences.

But to do so is to take a blinkered view of the world around us. One where we zoom in and in and in to our individual needs, wants and worries until we can see precious little else. This leads us to view our immediate, personal world as all-encompassing. In a very real way, we completely lose perspective.

Here's how Marcus puts it in Book 7:

According to Plato (and a whole bunch of people who've been up to space), anyone who wants to make pronouncements about the world should look down on events from way up above.

Peace. War. Loving. Hating. Births. Deaths. Family. Foreigners. People of every kind doing every kind of thing.

From this vantage point, it's all one crazy harmonious mix. **(Book 7, Meditation 48)**

Or for a more up-to-date example, Edgar Mitchell, Apollo 14 astronaut, put it this way:

In outer space you develop an instant global consciousness, a people orientation, an intense dissatisfaction with the state of the world, and a compulsion to do something about it. From out there on the Moon, international politics look so petty.

Once we understand that we are intimately part of a far, far larger whole, our own personal issues won't seem quite so big anymore. We'll tend to develop greater compassion for those around us – people who are far more like us than they are different. We will be more likely to take better care of our planet – after all, as my mum would say when I did something wrong, 'You're only hurting yourself.'

Marcus would say that the universe wants you to do the right thing, that you should act in accordance with the laws of nature. These laws, in his view, are always for the best for the whole of humanity (and the wider universe for that matter). They are not in themselves good or bad, they simply are what they are.

In itself, the universe is a pretty docile place. It doesn't hate you. It's not out to get you. When you think about things this way, it's easy to see that the natural laws that govern everything around us aren't evil. They don't make mistakes. They harm nothing. And ultimately, it's these same laws that govern everything that happens to us from birth to death. **(Book 6, Meditation 1)**

In a world where far too many of us are too eager to grab a slice of victimhood, this is a sobering thought.

As briefly mentioned earlier, Marcus also views what happens in the universe as a long series of repeating cycles – a version of 'what goes around comes around'. He says that you'll see nothing fundamentally different than all the people who've come before you (and your descendants will see nothing different in their turn).

We have a tendency to think of our problems as uniquely ours, as if they have been specially selected by fate to single us out for some pain and misery. But for Marcus, these problems are as old as time. As he points out later in Book 6:

> *To see the present is to see everything that's been before and everything that's yet to come because everything is linked.* **(Book 6, Meditation 37)**

So, again, why get stressed obsessing over the next crisis when the same thing has happened again and again (and will happen again and again)?

You are better off simply focusing on what you can do, right here, right now – with reason, fairness and common humanity front and centre in your mind. As Marcus explains at the start of Book 4:

> *When you're OK with the way things are in reality, you can adapt to whatever the world throws at you – threat or opportunity. You won't come at things weighed down by the baggage of expectation or prejudice. You'll be able to step back and get some distance. Then, no matter what happens, you can judge whether to embrace it, fight it or ignore it.* **(Book 4, Meditation 1)**

And that's really at the core of Stoicism. The Stoics would say that to lead a flourishing life, you simply need to separate reality from fantasy. You need to appreciate that you have very little control over the vast majority of stuff that happens around you. All you can ultimately do is try your best, acting with compassion for others, attempting to make the world a better place and refusing to take it personally if it doesn't work out.

MAKING IT WORK FOR YOU – FIVE KEY QUESTIONS

1. What issues in your life seem to happen over and over? How did you deal with them last time? How should you change your approach next time?

2. When have you felt that fate has had it in for you? How else could you have looked at this?

3. How do your expectations shape how you act? If you were to act without expecting a particular result, what would change?

4. Try altering your perspective – imagine looking down from an airplane flying overhead or further out to the view from the International Space Station – how does this change how you view issues, problems and the world around you?

5. How can this sense of interconnectedness foster greater compassion in how you view others?

THE MEDITATIONS

THE SECOND BOOK

> *'You are going to die. Right now, you're living on borrowed time. So why do you keep putting things off? Use every day to its fullest. Suck the marrow out of life. Because when your time's up, that's it, you don't get a second go.'*

1. SOME PEOPLE ARE DICKS

Let's face it, on pretty much any day, you'll come across people who'll try your patience. They may be rude or ignorant. They may lie to you or try to trick you. They may just be dicks.

Often, this is because they don't realise that they are, in fact, dicks. They can't get their heads around the difference between being a good, honest, reasonable person and being an annoying, self-centred jerk.

Thing is though, at some level, all these people are your brothers or sisters. Sure, you may not share parents or siblings or even the same country, but we all share the same essential humanity.

Now, you can decide to be hurt or offended by their words or actions, but that is *your* choice. Ultimately, however, we all need to be able to live and work together. It's simply the natural order of things. So get over it.

2. 60% WATER

What are we all really made of? A little flesh. Some breath in and out. And a chunk of grey matter that runs the show (more or less).

But your flesh is nothing of real concern. It's just a bunch of muscles, veins, blood and bones held together with some fancy wiring. Your breath comes and goes. It sucks. It blows. So what?

Now the grey matter, that's where the real stuff happens. Why then squander it getting trapped by every selfish whim, every little distraction? Too many people waste precious time moaning about the present or worrying about the future.

You're a long time dead, make the time you have count.

3. CHANGE HAPPENS
You may believe that some god or divine spirit controls the universe. Alternatively, you might think it's all down to chance and evolution. Whatever your view, it's pretty obvious that the world around you is the greater sum of a range of interconnected parts (no matter who or what drives it).

What's more, it's changing all the time. In fact, it's this change that makes pretty much everything else possible. You are a part of this, there are no bystanders in this game. You'll change the world around you just as surely as it'll change you. So don't sweat it.

4. TICK, TICK
You are going to die. Right now, you're living on borrowed time. So why do you keep putting things off? Use every day to its fullest. Suck the marrow out of life. Because when your time's up, that's it, you don't get a second go.

5. CUT THE CAT PICTURES
Whatever you're doing, focus. Do one thing and only one thing. Don't get distracted by all the crap around you. Ignore your phone, your social newsfeed, your addiction to the next shiny new thing. Get on with the task at hand with a positive mind and a good attitude.

Do this and you'll realise just how simple living a good life can be.

6. R-E-S-P-E-C-T
Isn't it time you showed yourself some respect? We only have one life and it could end tomorrow. If you don't respect yourself, your happiness will end up a hostage to what other people think about you.

7. WHY WORRY?
With every new thing that pops into your newsfeed, there is a fresh opportunity to worry about something that's totally out of your control (assuming you're not a world leader). Why play this game? It'll exhaust you and you'll almost certainly lose.

Instead, take time to learn something new. Something useful and interesting. Something that'll leave no room for pointless worry.

8. THINK OF A NUMBER
You're not a mind reader. Too many people get all wound up because they can't work out what others are really thinking. Yet in reality, the source of your unhappiness has more to do with a failure to understand how your own mind works.

9. BIG MEET SMALL

Here's something to focus on. The universe is big. Really, really big. And you are small. Tiny in fact. But however small you are, you're an inseparable part of the wider mass of everything. And no one can stop you saying or doing what's in total harmony with the wider universe.

10. GRADING ARSEHOLES

Some people act like arseholes because they're angry. Some because they want something (power, sex, stuff). There's an important difference.

The angry people are often in pain and struggle to control their actions. They suffer twice, once with perceived injustice and then again with the pain of their own response.

Those driven by desire are more self-seeking and calculating. They know that what they're doing is wrong and do it anyway.

So, ultimately, it's worse to be driven by desire than by anger.

11. READY TO DIE?

You should always behave like your next breath will be your last. If there is a god of some sort, you've got nothing to fear anyway. If there isn't (or they simply don't care about us mere mortals), then forget them.

We've evolved to deal with all sorts of challenges, why assume this all falls apart at death? You're probably more ready to face your end than you realise.

11½. NOTHING IS GOOD. NOTHING IS BAD.

In the real world, good and bad things happen to good and bad people in pretty much equal measure. Life and death. Riches and poverty. Pain and pleasure. And more often than not, these events don't change that person in the slightest.

So when you think about it, none of these things is, in its own right, either good or bad.

12. SO WHAT?

Everything in life is fleeting. It doesn't matter whether it's something that promises pleasure, something that threatens pain or something that inflates our sense of self-importance. Ultimately, when you consider what these mean in the wider span of the universe, it's all pretty inconsequential.

12½. DON'T FEAR THE REAPER

When you really look at it, death is about as natural as things get. You might as well fear the sun coming up. In fact, death is not just a natural event, it also helps keep the whole of nature working by recycling much-needed atoms.

13. GETTING OUT OF YOUR HEAD?

It's kind of sad when you see people going around in circles trying to get into other people's heads. The truth is, the only head you really need to get into is your own. Once you know your own mind, you can be calm, focused and at peace with the world.

14. NO TIME LIKE THE PRESENT

It doesn't matter whether you live for three thousand years or thirty thousand, all you really ever have is the present moment, same as everyone else.

You can't lose the past, it's already gone.

You can't gain the future, it's not here yet (and may never be).

Ultimately, there are two truths in all this. The first is that everything from the beginning of time is just a bunch of repeating patterns – you can keep watching them go round and round but they're all the same. The second is that no matter if you die young or old, all you ever lose is the present moment – and even this is not really yours to own.

15. AN ASS OF YOU AND ME

At the end of the day, we're ruled by our assumptions. Of course, you may disagree in your special case (surely this only applies to others). But at least consider the possibility that it's true.

16. PRESSING SELF-DESTRUCT

Call it your 'soul', call it your 'self', call it what you like. Whatever is the essential *youness* of you, there are a bunch of ways it can become cancerous to your wellbeing.

You can bitch and moan about the nature of the universe (it ain't going to change for you my special snowflake).

You can take against others and try to do them harm (what goes around comes around).

You can surrender control when faced by pleasure or pain (get a grip).

You can present a false picture of yourself to the world (how are your Instagram updates looking?).

Or you can do random shit, wasting your time on stuff that's meaningless (what's the point?).

17. LET'S GET REAL
What are you really?

The universe has been around for billions of years. You are a mere speck upon a speck. You are a simple collection of atoms held together in a fleshy bag of fluid. Your perception is, at best, a bit wonky and your mind is often all over the place. Your future is, let's face it, impossible to predict.

When it comes down to it, your body is like a fast-flowing river, always changing. Your thoughts are just smoke and mirrors. Your life is like an ongoing war in a foreign land. And when your time is up, oblivion awaits.

Sounds a bit sucky I know. So, is there nothing that can help you get through it?

The answer is philosophy. By this I don't mean some convoluted garbage in a never-read book. I mean the kind of thinking that protects your soul, self, spirit (or whatever you call it). The kind that frees you from being governed by pain and pleasure. That stops you doing random stuff for the sake of it.

It's the kind of philosophy that understands that shit happens and prepares us for our ultimate demise without freaking anyone out. It knows that when you shuffle off this mortal coil, it's just a way of Mother Nature redistributing your atoms – so why worry about it?

After all, those atoms were around long before you made use of them and will carry on being useful until the end of the universe.

THE THIRD BOOK

> *'Life is tough. If it gives you anything beyond justice, truth, wisdom and courage, then carpe the diem out of it.'*

1. GET ON WITH IT

Time is running out for all of us. While you might want to live to a ripe old age, even if you do, chances are that your mind won't be as sharp as it used to be.

Sure, your body may hold up OK (more or less), but if your mind starts to go south, you'll struggle to keep everything together, to make the best decisions, to get stuff done.

So what are you waiting for? It's not just that the Grim Reaper may show up at any minute, do the stuff that matters while your mind is up to the job.

2. GO DEEPER

There's something really pleasing about the natural world. It's not perfect, of course. There are cracks and blemishes all over the place. But when you see things in their natural setting, they just look right.

So, when you look around you, don't get taken in by perfection (it's probably just Photoshopped anyway). Look deeper. Enjoy every last wonder the real world has to offer.

3. DEAD CLEVER

No matter how clever Einstein was, he didn't outsmart death. James Dean was a great actor and left a fine-looking corpse. By all accounts, Princess Diana was a lovely woman who did great things for charity (until her untimely end in a tunnel in Paris).

So what's the point?

Simply this: You get on board, you travel, you arrive (sooner or later). After that, who knows? If you believe in any sort of god, hopefully they'll be waiting. If not, all your cares and troubles will be at an end anyway.

4. NEVER HEARD OF THEM

Don't waste your time obsessing over others unless it's to some sort of mutual advantage for you both (face it, they probably won't read your tweet and certainly won't remember it an hour later). Just think what else you could use this time for. So ditch this kind of thinking and focus on the important stuff.

Get to the point where if someone suddenly asks, *'What are you thinking about?'* you can immediately give an answer that shows that you're a simple, kind person with no time for the rubbish that fills so many people's heads.

It'll demonstrate that you're not ruled by petty distractions, that you are content with whatever the world throws at you, that you just don't care what others are saying or thinking or doing.

Achieve this and you'll be able to stay focused on doing some good in the world, whether it's to fulfil your own destiny (no matter how grand or modest) or help others navigate the choppy waters of life.

And as for all those celebs, attention junkies and energy vampires that suck up so much attention? Screw them.

5. WHEN YOU ACT, ACT

Don't do anything you're not willing to do. Avoid acting on the spur of the moment. And when you do act, give it your all – don't be half-hearted.

Don't waste your time talking up what you're going to do. Say just what you mean and do what you say you will.

We all play many roles: parent, child, friend, lover, boss, employee. Play them all without expecting praise or validation from others. And smile damn it!

Make it clear that you don't need anyone's help, that you can stand on your own two feet and don't need propping up by others.

6. DO THE RIGHT THING

Life is tough. If it gives you anything beyond justice, truth, wisdom and courage, then carpe the diem out of it.

On the flip side, if it gives you nothing but your ability to rely on yourself and your own mind for guidance, then ignore all the other crap that'll distract you from being your best self.

These distractions will kill you – no matter whether it's getting 10,000 followers on Instagram, making a million, or getting laid in ways there isn't even a Pornhub category for.

You may think these are all part of you fulfilling your potential, but they're not. Listen to me, just do the right thing.

Now, you might reply, *'They sound pretty alright to me.'* And they might. But take the time to look a little deeper. Are they really going to make you the best person you can be? Only you can say.

7. STORING UP TROUBLE

It might not seem like it at the time, but no good will come from doing anything right now that will result in you having to lie or suspect others' motives or lose your self-respect.

If you can keep your rational self front and centre at all times, you won't need to pretend to be something you're not or moan about your lot in life or crave either company or solitude.

You won't worry about how much longer you'll be on this Earth. In fact, if you got wiped out by the proverbial lightning bolt tomorrow, you'd check out with a clear conscience, knowing you stuck to the right path.

8. GET SOME DISCIPLINE

A disciplined mind is a beautiful thing. In it you'll find none of the mental junk that poisons so much of everyday life. The person who achieves this discipline will neither grovel for approval nor think they are top dog. They will neither depend on others nor be afraid of asking for help. Ultimately, they'll answer to no one but themselves.

9. BEWARE FAKE OPINIONS

Be careful how you form your opinions. It's your one defence against making assumptions built on poor foundations. Check your sources –

just because it's on your newsfeed, doesn't mean it's true (no matter how much you'd like it to be). Take time over this and you'll get on better with those around you (or at the very least, be immune to their nonsense).

10. RIGHT HERE, RIGHT NOW

If you take little else from what I say, take this: We live only in the present moment. The rest is either done and dusted or is something yet to come (and won't turn out the way you expect anyway).

In the greater scheme of things, our lives are small, played out on a tiny patch of a blue speck floating through the cosmos. And fame? That's bullshit. It's just selective memories by people who'll soon be dead themselves.

If that doesn't put things into perspective, I don't know what will.

11. ASK THE RIGHT QUESTIONS

Whenever you see or think anything, strip it down in your mind to its bare essentials. Give it a name, a simple description. Name all its parts.

Doing this will build some serious mental strength. It'll help you work out what you're dealing with, where it fits into the world around you, and whether you should spend any more time on it.

You can go further and ask yourself a series of questions.

Why is this thing here now?

What's it made of?

How long will it last?

What will it demand of you?

Is it here by some random chance?

Or is it the result of human activity?

12. GIVE IT EVERYTHING YOU'VE GOT
Whatever you do, stay focused and give it your all. Expect nothing and fear nothing – simply do what you believe to be right. If you can do this, you'll have a good life. What's more, no one will be able to stop you.

13. THE RIGHT TOOLS FOR THE JOB
In the same way that a surgeon will have all the instruments they need within reach, ready to save a life, you should always have your principles to hand, ready to learn more about the world and people around you. And never forget that everything is in some way interconnected.

14. I LOVE YOU TOMORROW?
All those books you plan to read. Those tabs you have open for later. That bucket list of experiences to try before you die (someday, maybe). Do it now while there's still time. You're a long time dead.

15. SEE THIS
People are blind. They can't see what it really means to steal, to plant, to consume, to be at peace, to do the right thing. That's because to really see

these things demands a different kind of vision than what their eyes can provide.

16. WE'RE ALL THE SAME. WE'RE ALL DIFFERENT.

We're all a mix of body, soul and mind. The body for physical sensations. The soul or self for our impulse to act. And the mind for our core principles.

But we also share our capacity for physical sensations with every wild animal and burrowing parasite on the planet. Every nutjob, tyrant or internet troll is driven by impulse. And even terrorists, paedophiles and Fox News pundits have minds to guide them.

With so much in common, what separates a good person from the rest?

Well, it's the fact that they can embrace the whims of fate without resorting to irrational thinking and kneejerk reactions. It's in their ability to face up to the real world without resorting to lies or taking advantage of others. It's in the way they refuse to be put off when others question how they can live such simple, self-respecting, happy lives.

THE FOURTH BOOK

> 'Love what you do. Enjoy your talents. They'll allow you to spend the rest of your life as neither master nor slave.'

1. GET SOME PERSPECTIVE
When you're OK with the way things are in reality, you can adapt to whatever the world throws at you – threat or opportunity. You won't come at things weighed down by the baggage of expectation or prejudice. You'll be able to step back and get some distance. Then, no matter what happens, you can judge whether to embrace it, fight it or ignore it.

2. THERE IS NO TRY
Yoda was right. If you're going to do something, do it properly and with purpose.

3. WISH YOU WERE HERE?
Everyone wants to get away from it all to the perfect hideaway.

Ever notice how it's almost always somewhere far away? Thing is, get your mind into the right place and you can get away from it all without ever leaving your own head. Understand your own mind and you can find this inner peace whenever you want, as often as you like.

In doing so, you can recharge your batteries whenever you feel run down (just make sure you don't take too long to get back in the game).

What really stresses you out anyway? Other people? Remember, we're all in this together, tolerating others is just part of creating a fair world. People aren't willingly evil. And whatever they do wrong will soon be gone (as will they before they know it). So chill out.

Maybe it's your personal circumstances that make you worry. Well, either we're just a random jumble of atoms or there is some wider purpose to all this. If it's random, what can you do except roll with the punches? If there is purpose, then simply play your part to the best of your ability.

Or are you hurting? Well, pain is simply what the brain determines it to be. Train your mind to detach from the physical and you'll hurt a lot less.

Or are you worried about what others think of you? Not getting enough love for your latest Instagram update? Soon enough, no one will either remember nor care. You're on a tiny part of a small blue dot flying through the universe. When you look at it from that perspective, who gives a damn what others think?

So take a break in the sanctuary of your mind when you need to. Whatever happens, view things from the perspective of a human who is on this planet for just a little while. When it comes to it, nothing outside your mind can really affect you (unless you let it). And when shit happens, it won't last long anyway.

Let's face it, most run-of-the-mill bad stuff has happened to you loads of times in the past and you probably remember hardly any of it. Why will this one be any different?

In the final analysis, everything changes and most things in life are simply a matter of opinion.

4. HELLO FELLOW CITIZEN
We all have minds, we're all rational creatures, we can all tell right from wrong. It doesn't matter where you're from, we're all citizens of planet Earth. From this fellow citizenship, we all get our understanding, reason and law. Nothing comes from nothing – the mind is no different.

5. THE LOVE LIFE OF ATOMS
Birth. Death. It's all part of the same process – atoms come together, atoms break apart. There's nothing really to get worked up about, it's just part of nature.

6. SPARE CHANGE
You can't change people, they'll act as they will. Expecting anything different is like expecting a cat to bark. But why worry? Soon we'll be dead and a little while later, no one will remember us anyway.

7. GET OVER IT
Don't get all wound up and offended by others. Abandon the feeling of being wronged and you'll get rid of the wrong itself.

8. BECOME BULLETPROOF
What doesn't affect your mind can't affect your life or harm you in any way.

9. THE WHOLE ENCHILADA
Ultimately, the natural course of action is one that benefits the whole of humanity, nature and the universe.

10. GET IN ORDER
Whatever you do should be the result of an ordered series of decisions (not just a random bunch of events). Make sure your heart is in the right place. Do the right thing, not just the easy one, and you won't go far wrong.

11. GET A REALITY CHECK
How you view the world will dictate your opinions. So be careful to see it as it really is and not as it appears on Facebook or in the news or how you'd like it to be.

12. A SIMPLE RECIPE
OK, two things. First, do only what reason says is good for those around you. Second, don't be afraid to change your mind if (and only if) someone can convince you based on reason and the common good.

13. A REASONABLE IDEA?
You've got a brain right? Then why not use it? Once you can apply reason to all your problems, you've got life nailed.

14. AN ATOM AT A TIME
You are a part of the universe, and at some point, you'll dissolve back into it, atom by atom.

15. A HAIKU
Many petals fall
Some fall now and some later
There's no difference

16. HOW AWESOME ARE YOU?
Right now, some people may see you as a bit of an idiot. (I know, right?) But get back in touch with your reason and in a week's time they'll see you as some kind of god.

17. THE SAND IS RUNNING DOWN
Face it, you won't live to be a thousand. Time's running out for you just like everyone else. Do some good while you still can.

18. GO STRAIGHT AHEAD
Don't waste time caring about what others say or do. Just focus on doing the right thing. Not only will it cut down stress, you'll get where you need to go faster.

19. THE DEAD DON'T REMEMBER
So many people want to be remembered for something after they've died. But really, who cares?

Say people do remember you, soon they'll be dead too. So will those that come after them. And even if, by some miracle of science, they did live forever, what's it to you? Nothing.

Face it, in all your desire to make your mark for posterity, you're wasting what you could be doing today.

20. FLATTERY WILL GET YOU NOWHERE
Truly beautiful things are beautiful whether anyone praises them or not. It's the same with intelligence or kindness or talent. In reality, none of these things is ever improved by praise or damaged by criticism.

21. WE ARE ALL MADE OF STARS
Is there really a way for the soul to go on after death?

If there is a heaven, wouldn't it get full? Think about all those physical bodies – people and animals – buried in the earth or that have gone up in smoke. They've simply transformed from one collection of atoms to another.

So maybe whatever we think of as a soul will go through the same process, transforming back into the stardust that makes up the universe around us.

How can we know the truth? By understanding the difference between things and the evidence for what happens.

22. IT'S SIMPLE REALLY
Stop fucking about. Simply make sure you're seeing what's really there and do the right thing.

23. WHAT GOES AROUND COMES AROUND
It's like this: Things will happen when they happen – no sooner, no later.

Ultimately, everything comes from nature and, sooner or later, everything ends up there too.

24. FREE: TIME
In the real world, it's better to do a few things well than try to do anything and everything.

Most of the other stuff is just bullshit anyway. So you might as well save yourself the time and trouble. Whenever you're faced with another to-do, ask yourself, *'Is this really necessary?'* If not, don't even think about it.

25. TAKE THIS TEST
Try this on for size: Simply attempt to lead a good life. Be happy with your lot. Enjoy doing the right thing. Then see how it suits you.

26. TAKE A CHILL PILL
Chill out. Unfaze yourself. If someone you know is doing wrong, that's their problem. If something has happened to you, so what? That's just the way the cookie crumbles.

Life is short my friend. Seize the moment. Don't get caught up with things you can do nothing about.

27. MAYBE YOU'RE NOT AS CRAZY AS YOU THINK YOU ARE
Either the universe is an interconnected orderly affair or it's the chaos of an angry two-year-old. Thing is, can there be so much disorder in the universe and still order within you? Think about it – everything around you in nature simply works.

28. RANT

What an absolute dick! What a muggle-brained, stubborn, small-minded fool! (Sorry, sometimes you've just got to let it out.)

29. GETTING CUT OFF

Those who fail to see the true world around them are as much a stranger to reality as those who are simply a bit dim. They are exiled. Blind. Poor. Birdshit on the newly cut hair of the world – a world they've divorced by bitching about 'stuff' (while forgetting that they are just 'stuff' themselves). It's like they've amputated themselves from a world where everything should be one.

30. SOMETIMES, REASON IS ALL THERE IS

Philosophers are a funny sort. You get one without a coat, another without books. One will complain about having no food but say they still have faith in reason. For my part, while I make no money from my learning, I'll still stick with it.

31. NOBODY'S SLAVE

Love what you do. Enjoy your talents. They'll allow you to spend the rest of your life as neither master nor slave.

32. NOT WORTH A BEAN

Look back in history. Take the 60s for example. All those people going about their lives: getting married, having kids, getting sick, dying, fighting, partying, doing business, throwing insults, having sex, making money, chasing power.

Fast forward to the 80s and you'll see exactly the same thing.

Today? Just the same again.

All those people throughout history beavering away before passing away. You probably know some yourself, running headlong after their little vanities rather than focusing on the simple good life that lies right at their feet.

At the end of the day, things are only worth what they're actually worth. Remember this and you won't get distracted.

33. NO ONE THINKS ABOUT BETAMAX ANYMORE

Words go out of fashion and die – who today talks about video cassettes or modems or velocipedes? It is the same for people – the stars of our childhoods fade over time. Even an Elvis Presley or a Princess Diana is spoken about less today than in their time. Even the mega-famous and super powerful are destined to become footnotes in history.

Let's face it, what good is everlasting fame to anyone? Nothing. Zero. Zilch. So why bother?

What makes life worth living? Just this: understanding the world, doing the right thing, telling the truth and cultivating an attitude that treats every event as no big thing.

34. GIVE IT UP

Give yourself over to whatever happens and play your part in the rich tapestry of life.

35. FORGET ABOUT IT
Everything is just dust in the wind – both the person who remembers and the person remembered.

36. PLANT A SEED
If one thing is certain, it's change. One thing leads to another and another and another. You think the only seeds are the ones that develop into plants? Think again.

37. RIP
You'll soon be dead. Yet you still worry. You're still afraid. You still rush to take on other people's troubles. What's the point?

38. SCHOOL'S IN
Check out what really makes wise people tick. What do they love? What do they hate?

39. HEAD TO HEAD
What goes on in other people's heads can't harm you. So why do you hurt? It's simply because, in your own head, you've decided you're harmed.

It's the same with physical pain. Refuse the judgement and you'll eliminate the pain.

What happens in life is neither good nor bad, it's thinking that makes it so

40. ALL STUFF AND NONSENSE
Remember, everything in the universe is made of the same stuff – atoms. More than this, it's all interconnected. Everything affects everything else – like the butterfly in South America that sets in train events that become a hurricane thousands of miles away.

41. AS EPICTETUS PUT IT...
'You are just a soul lugging a corpse.'

42. CHANGE FOR GOOD?
Change isn't necessarily a bad thing. But then again, the outcome of change isn't always good either (no matter what the self-help gurus say).

43. SINK OR SWIM
Time is like a river in full flood. No sooner do you get a grip on what's happening than it is swept past to be replaced by the next thing, and the next, and the next.

44. IT'S ONLY NATURAL
Everything is as natural as spring flowers or summer fruit. This includes sickness, death, lies, office politics and the popularity of cat pics on the internet – everything that delights and everything that brings misery.

45. CAUSE THEN EFFECT (REPEAT)
Whatever occurs always follows on from what happened before. It's not just a random hodgepodge of events but an orderly sequence of cause and effect. Just as everything that already exists works as part of the whole,

everything new takes its place in the great cosmic clockwork too.

46. AS HERACLITUS PUT IT…
'When earth dies, water is born. When water expires, air is born. And when air kicks the bucket, we get fire. And on and on.'

He also talked about *'people who've forgotten where their paths are heading'* and about *'people who are strangers to their constant companion: reason.'*

Ultimately, he advises us all to avoid sleepwalking into the future and to refuse to simply act as obedient children just because that's what others do.

47. WHAT ARE YOU DOING TOMORROW?
Imagine there is a god and they say to you, *'Tomorrow, you're going to die. Or if not tomorrow, definitely the day after.'* Will you really make a huge fuss over which it's to be?

Thing is, in the greater scheme of things, the same applies if we're talking days, months or years. So treat it all the same and stop worrying.

48. THIS IS A ONE-WAY TRIP
Never forget how many doctors have died – men and women who spent their careers pondering their patients' illnesses. Or the many futurologists who predicted impending doom. Or all the philosophers who've come up with grand theories about life and death. Or the millions of soldiers who've killed for whatever cause. Or the politicians who thought up the cause in the first place. In fact, think of all the towns and cities that have been destroyed over the ages.

Then count up all the people you've known personally who've buried and mourned their friends only to be buried and mourned themselves not so long after.

Existence is quick and dangerous (and nobody makes it out alive). From a tumble in the sheets to a corpse in the coffin, it goes faster than we imagine. So live your life on your terms. And then, when your number is up, go with good grace, ready to return to the pool of atoms that makes up the whole of the universe.

49. DO YOU FEEL LUCKY?

Be like the rock (the stone, not the actor) that stands in the sea, pounded by the waves, yet standing firm.

Now you could get all sulky with a *'Man, I'm so unlucky'* vibe. But don't.

Instead, go with, *'How lucky am I that I can take all this shit and still stand and face it.'* Just think, others may have simply given up. Not you.

And what is luck anyway?

Why do we choose to call this one thing bad luck and this other good luck? If it is just how things turn out in the real world, then luck has nothing to do with it. Does whatever happened stop you from being fair, forgiving, truthful, kind, well-meaning, independent and all those other things that will enable you to live up to your full potential?

So the next time you're tempted to bitch about your bad luck, think this: Enduring 'bad luck' and coming successfully out the other side is actually good luck. Lucky you.

50. A GOOD INNINGS?

OK, let's park the whole philosophy thing for a minute.

You're afraid of dying, I get it. Try this for size: Think of all those old people who staved off the Reaper for longer than most but are now pushing up daisies. Are they better off than those who didn't manage 'a good innings'?

Sure, they got a few more years of work. A few more years of hanging out with tolerable people. A few more years encased in a failing body.

Maybe that's a good thing, but still, they all ended up dead just like everyone else.

When you think about the 13.8 billion years to date and the probable infinity of years to come, there's not much difference between a centenarian with a weak bladder and a baby that doesn't make it out of the hospital.

51. DO NOT PASS GO

Always take the shortest, simplest route. It'll free you from unnecessary stress and drama, allowing you to make the right choices and act accordingly.

THE FIFTH BOOK

> *'Don't wallow in self-pity. Don't lust after every new fad or gadget. Don't bitch and whine. Don't be <u>that</u> person.'*

1. GET OUT OF BED!
Can't get out of bed? Tempted by a duvet day? Tell yourself this: *'I'm getting up to do my thing. To get shit done. No point being a wimp. It's time to fulfil my potential and the duvet ain't helping.'*

'Oh, but it's so comfy and warm,' I hear you say.

Really? I'm happy for you. But do you really think your place in the universe is to snuggle duvets rather than embracing all the world has to offer?

Look around you. Look at the sparrows, the ants, the bees, the plants even. They're not wallowing in oh-dear-poor-me. They're getting on with it, sparrowing, anting, beeing and planting all over the place.

That's because they accept that they're part of the whole interconnected universe around them.

'But it's natural to rest too,' I hear you say (muffled from under the duvet no doubt).

Sure. But we all have a natural rest period just like we have a natural amount of food and drink we need each day. But you're overdoing it. I bet you're quick enough to set limits and stick to them when it comes to real work.

Do you hate yourself so much that you're not willing to be the best you can be?

Find something you love, do it well, do it better every single day. Get this right and it'll absorb you, pulling you out of bed at first light and dropping you back there with a smile on your face at the end of the day.

Importantly, it's not about the money. This is about making the world around you a better place.

Get on with it.

2. PEACE OUT
Once you manage to get rid of all the crap in your head, inner peace is child's play.

3. YOU BE YOU
If it's correct, true and fair, you've got every right to say or do anything you damn well please.

Ignore what others say, tweet or post about you. If you're doing the right thing, a bit of criticism doesn't matter. Others will follow their own consciences. That's not your problem. Your path and that of the universe around you are one and the same.

4. UNTIL MY LAST DAY

I'll carry on doing the right thing until I breathe my last. After that, all the atoms that are part of me will return to the universe that supplied my father's seed and my mother's milk. I'll become part of the same Earth that has fed and watered me, that has put up with my footsteps and endured my abuse.

5. PULL YOUR FINGER OUT

So you're not the sharpest tool in the box, so what? That's no excuse.

Work on your strengths. Work on the things that you can control: honesty, sincerity, never giving up.

Don't wallow in self-pity. Don't lust after every new fad or gadget. Don't bitch and whine. Don't be *that* person.

Can't you see that everything you've got going for you? Can't you see that you can do so much more with what you've got? Don't hide your talents just because they're not the ones the media values the highest.

And if you want to work on your weaknesses, then work on them. There's nothing there that can't be improved if you're willing to put in the effort.

6. ONE, TWO OR THREE?

There are three types of people in the world. There are those that are quick to loudly demand repayment for every little favour. Then there are those that, while quieter, keep score in their heads and are only too aware of what they think they're owed. Finally, there are those who never think about what they've done for others, it's just how their worlds work. In the same way a bee produces honey, they help others. It's no big thing.

Be that third type.

'But shouldn't I get credit for my actions?' you say. 'Isn't that the rational thing to do?'

You're not getting it. You're just jumping into bed with the first two.

If you really get my meaning, you'll never have to worry about failing to do the right thing just because you're too busy looking for a reward.

7. THOU ART TALKING BOLLOCKS

'Hey Zeus, how about a bit of rain?' If we're going to pray, let's keep it simple. No god is going to be impressed by your Shakespeare impression.

8. A TOUGH PILL TO SWALLOW?

So your doctor tells you to stay hydrated and prescribes a course of antibiotics. Fair enough. Of course, flip this round and we could say nature has prescribed some disease, disfigurement or disability. The former prescription is about making you better, the latter about fulfilling your destiny.

Think of it like a fine stone wall, all the blocks fitting neatly together to make something whole and solid. It's the result of a series of events fitting together just so to deliver a certain outcome.

We might say, 'So-and-so had it coming' and yes, they did. Just as we accept our doctor's prescription (even if the medicine tastes foul), we should also accept what the world serves up. It's just part of the way of things.

In fact, there are two reasons why you should chill out about what happens to you. The first is that it is the inevitable result of a whole series of events seen and unseen that was always going to end at precisely this point in time. The second is that these events are part of the universe, and to change what's happened to date is to break the whole (good luck with that).

So quit bitching about it.

9. YOU'RE GOING TO SCREW UP
OK, so you're trying to follow the whole Stoicism thing. Great, but every now and then you're going to fall short (or even royally fuck it up).

Relax.

Simply go back to the core ideas, use reason as your guide and realise that most of your actions are those of a good person. If you love the ideas, don't slink back like a naughty child who's been told off. Return with a spring in your step like you're being reunited with an old friend.

Don't make some huge song and dance about it. At the end of the day, this is a philosophy that's about you gaining the inner peace of someone who follows their best nature.

Now you might say, *'Cool, so it's all about what makes me happy.'*

Well, yes, but watch out. There are a whole bunch of things that can make you happy on the surface, but you have to ask yourself, wouldn't real happiness come from being free, kind, open and honest? Wouldn't you be happier knowing what to do in any given situation?

10. FAKE NEWS

Can you ever really know anything for sure?

It seems we live in an age of fake-everything. Whatever you hear one week, is 'disproved' the next.

But back in the real world, aren't we all fallible? Our experiences are fleeting, and there's no end of scammers and conmen who are keen to pray on us. Ever those closest to us can become a bit of a pain. (In truth, who hasn't tired of their own ridiculousness from time to time?)

With all this sound and fury, who should any of us pay attention to?

Surely it's better to simply wait for our inevitable end without getting bent out of shape. In doing so, consider two thoughts. The first is that things will happen as they happen (with very little influence from any of us). The second is that, if we so choose, there is no power on Earth that can make us act against our personal truths.

11. WHAT'S YOUR HEAD UP TO?

'What's my mind up to - right here, right now?'

It's a good question. One you should ask regularly.

Who's really in control? A child? A tyrant? Some animal driven solely by instinct?

Who?

12. LEADING THE GOOD LIFE

When we talk about 'goods' what do we really mean?

These days, all too often we mean stuff – things that are bought and sold. The kind of stuff that, when we overindulge, leads to the old phrase *'too much of a good thing.'*

But if you think about 'goods' in terms of wisdom, courage, justice, doing the right thing, then having too much of a good thing won't mean anything.

13. ALL JUST ATOMS

When it comes down to it, we're all just made up of atoms. None of these will vanish when we're dead (just as none of them magically appeared out of nowhere when we were born). They'll simply be reused (upcycled even) into something else, and something else after that, on and on until the end of time.

It was the same for our parents, and theirs before them. It's just the way things are.

14. DIRECT TO THE POINT

Reason will simply do its own thing. It's got its own rules and ways. Once it gets going, you need to stand back and let it get on with it.

That's why we think of the right course of action as 'direct' – it's straight to the point and *directs* what we should do next.

15. BACK TO THE CORE

Nothing can ever really belong to you that's not core to your human nature. Nobody should expect anything else from you or claim anything else as your ultimate purpose in life.

If any of this external stuff was really core to who you are, you wouldn't be strengthened by doing without it. Whereas, in reality, the more you can do without all that fluff and nonsense, the better you'll feel.

16. THINK BETTER THOUGHTS

Your mind is coloured by the kind of thoughts it has.

So try to give it the right kind of thoughts to work with. Such as, *'It's always possible to live right'* – no matter if you live in a palace or out on the street.

Or how about, *'Things tend to evolve to be suited to their ultimate purpose'*? As humans, we've evolved as social animals. Living together in harmony is a big part of what we're about.

17. THIS IS NUTS

To want the impossible is madness – yet many people can't seem to do anything else.

18. STUPIDITY VS WISDOM

Nothing will happen that you can't handle.

You see others face the same problems as you and, either because they're clueless or simply want to avoid embarrassment, they don't let it get to them.

Surely you're not going to let their ignorance outperform your wisdom?

19. DON'T LET IT GET TO YOU
Whatever shit's going down in the world, it can't truly get inside, affect or move the mind. That's down to the mind itself. Ultimately, it's the mind alone that judges the importance of what happens around it.

20. WHAT OBSTACLE?
We all want to play nice with others, be kind, show a bit of patience. But when those same others try to stop us doing what's right, they become as indifferent to us as a breath of wind.

Of course, sometimes other people will stop you physically from doing something or other. But they can't stop your mind. They can't impede your will. That's because your mind can get past any obstruction.

More than this, your mind can turn obstacles into objectives and use barriers as battering rams.

21. 'NUF RESPECT
Respect the forces that drive the universe. But know that those forces are within you too. You are part of the same whole.

22. DON'T LOSE IT
If something doesn't harm society, it can't harm the individual.

So if you think you've been wronged, tell yourself, *'If the community around me isn't harmed, neither am I.'*

But what if those around you *are* harmed? Don't get angry at the culprit. Instead, help them understand where they got it so wrong.

23. PADDLING IN THE RIVER OF LIFE
Think about how often the stuff around you comes and goes in the blink of an eye. The great river of life is always flowing, always changing – nothing stands still. It flows from the infinity that lies behind us to the eternity that lies ahead.

When you think of it like that, it seems pretty silly to worry and rage. It'll all be over soon anyway.

24. WE'RE ALL NOTHING
Add up all the time that's ever been, all 13.8 billion years or so. Now work out your share of it. If you live to be 96 years old, it'll be just 0.0000007%. Pretty much nothing.

25. ISN'T THAT THEIR PROBLEM?
So, someone is an arsehole to me. So what? That's their problem, not mine. I'll just carry on doing my thing.

26. SINS OF THE FLESH
Don't let your body ambush your mind. Pain, pleasure, lust, whatever. Keep them separate.

Of course, this is easier said than done. But when your mind does engage with the flesh, accept what's happening without getting all judgemental about it.

27. ONE
Be at one with the universe. How? Be at peace with who you are, be true to yourself, glory in your mind and reason.

28. SILENT BUT DEADLY
Someone farts in an elevator, so what? Have you never let one go?

'Hold on,' you say, *'surely they knew that it'd be offensive.'*

Well aren't you clever? And since you're so smart, why not use your smarts to explain their error to them. But do so without getting all worked up about it, that's for another kind of arsehole.

29. CHECK-OUT TIME?
It's altogether possible to live on Earth as you'd like to in any imagined heaven. If others won't allow it, you are perfectly free to take the shortcut and quit this whole living thing altogether. No problem.

But until then, don't let anything or anyone stop you from living the life of your best self.

30. FORTY-TWO
The universe is social. Interconnected. Everything is mutually interdependent. At its best, everything just works.

31. A RETROSPECTIVE
Looking back, how have you treated those around you – your parents, teachers, friends, lovers?

Can you honestly say you've never done any of them wrong?

Think about everything you've gone through in your life. As your time comes to an end, think of all you've seen, the pleasures, the pains, the honours you refused, the people you treated fairly (even when they didn't deserve it).

32. CALL YOURSELF WISE?

Why do idiots confound the wise? Maybe a better question is, who is really wise? When it comes down to it, only the person who can see how reason runs throughout eternity.

33. WAITING FOR THE END

Pretty soon, you'll be just ashes and dust. A name that some people remember perhaps. Perhaps not.

Everything that people set their hearts on in life is little more than stuff and nonsense. All too often we act like toddlers – laughing one minute, sulking another, then throwing ourselves on the floor in the supermarket when we don't get what we want.

Decency and truth are nowhere to be seen. So why stay here when you know your senses are dim and easily fooled? When even a million social media likes mean absolutely nothing? What should you do?

Chill out. Keep calm. Wait for the end – whether that's death or some form of transformation.

But what about until then? Do good to others (no matter how they act towards you) and remember: Whatever is outside your body and mind isn't yours to own and owes you nothing at all.

34. PROSPERITY THIS WAY
Keep on keeping on, no matter what. Stay in control of your choices and actions and you'll prosper on your terms.

Two things are true for every rational being. The first is that you can resist whatever stands in your way. And the second is that real happiness stems from doing the right thing.

35. WHO CARES?
If a wrong is not your fault and society doesn't suffer as a result, who really cares?

36. NO HARM, NO FOUL
Don't get too dragged into others' problems. Help where you can, but if they're not really harmed, don't pretend that they are.

Just because someone is crying over things that don't ultimately matter, it doesn't mean you have to join them.

37. STAY LUCKY
Some people are fortunate, they lack nothing that matters. They die knowing that they had the best temperament, the best impulses and the best behaviour.

THE SIXTH BOOK

> *'Be at one with the universe around you.*
> *Love others unconditionally. Play nice.'*

1. THE UNIVERSE DOESN'T HATE YOU

In itself, the universe is a pretty docile place. It doesn't hate you. It's not out to get you. When you think about things this way, it's easy to see that the natural laws that govern everything around us aren't evil. They don't make mistakes. They harm nothing. And ultimately, it's these same laws that govern everything that happens to us from birth to death.

2. TO YOUR LAST BREATH

I'll say it again, do the right thing.

It doesn't matter whether you're freezing cold or dead on your feet. Nor whether you are being cheered on or beaten down. Or even whether you're living it large or drawing your last breath. See, even the act of dying is part of life and deserves your best efforts.

3. GO DEEP OR GO HOME

These days, too few people look beneath the surface. Don't be one of them. Look deeper to find the intrinsic worth in everything and everyone.

4. FIRE AND FLOOD
Everything around you will change – whether it comes to some fiery end or gently disintegrates into its component atoms.

5. GET OUT OF THE WAY
Reason knows what it's doing. More than this, it knows how to do it and why.

6. REVENGE
The best revenge? Don't be like them.

7. HAPPINESS STARTS HERE
If you focus on one source of joy in this world, let it be this: Be kind, help others, repeat.

8. CLARITY LIES WITHIN
The rational part of you has no problem understanding the world around you. It can take any form it likes. Fundamentally, it can do what it damn well pleases.

9. YOU ARE HERE
Everything works as it does within one interconnected universe. Face it, barring the discovery of wormholes or some such, there is no other universe. None.

10. ORDER VS CHAOS

We can either look at the world as a random collection of atoms bumping into one another or as an interconnected environment governed by order.

If we go with the former, why be so eager to struggle on prolonging a life that's destined to be forever chaotic and confusing? It's all going to turn to dust anyhow. In fact, why worry about even that?

Of course, if we go down the route of an ordered world, we can calmly accept that we're part of the bigger picture and get on with doing our bit.

11. SURFING THE SHITSTORM

When everything is getting too much – your friends are being annoying, your enemies are being even more shitty than usual, the dog has done who knows what on the carpet – turn inwards.

Get back in tune with who you are and what's really important. The more you do this, the easier it will become, and you'll be able to call on this inner peace whenever you need to.

12. NO EVIL STEPMOTHERS

Say you had both a stepmother and a mother at the same time. Sure, you'd treat your stepmother with respect (you would, wouldn't you?), but it'd always be your mum you'd go back to.

It's the same with society and philosophy. Keep going back to philosophy, it will refresh you and make living in this crazy world more bearable.

13. FISH CORPSE ANYONE?

So you enjoy a fancy meal, how nice. But think about it, on your plate is a dead fish or chicken or pig. The wine? Grape juice.

And what about sex? Some enjoyable friction ending in a bit of moaning and your O face (hopefully).

When you think about things this way, it cuts out all the bullshit. You see things for what they really are. And you can apply this to everything in life.

So when things are being hyped up, clouded in smoke and mirrors, you'll be able to lay them bare. And don't for a minute think you get out of this, it's just the same when you're tempted to believe your own hype too.

14. CHECK OUT THOSE THREADS

A lot of people will admire the stuff around them (fast cars, a nice watch, a killer pair of shoes). Others are more likely to admire people (the A-list actress, the current face of whatever fashion label is trending, the Instagram celeb with the impossible lifestyle). Others still will admire the products of talent and skill (great art and design, writing that speaks to you, films that move you to tears).

But in the end, if you really value reason above all else, you'll spend less time admiring such things and more time focusing on nurturing the core of who you really are and searching out others who think the same.

15. AND BREATHE

It seems some things can't wait to be born while others can't wait to die.

In fact, even when something is on the way in, part of it is often on the way out.

Change is endless. The universe is continually renewing itself around us as time flows by. But with all this swirling around you, how do you know what to focus on? It's like trying to get the number of that gorgeous creature you saw in the bar when they've already jumped in a cab and headed off into the dark.

But that's just the way it is. Life is simply a series of breaths. In and out. On and on. It's something you gained just yesterday at your birth and will give back when you inevitably die.

16. STRIP IT BACK

So what should we really care about? There are billions of different creatures on the planet, all breathing just like us, all with similar senses (some better, some worse), many are social, all need to feed – and all need to shit too. What makes us special?

Is it our desires, jumping and laughing and dancing at the drop of a hat? No.

What about the praise of others, the clapping of hands, the wagging of tongues, the hundreds of likes on our latest update? No again.

When it comes down to it, the only thing to really care about is acting in accordance with your true self – when everything else is stripped away – the core truth of what it is to be you.

It's the same with any tool or technology. It does precisely the job it was designed to do (whatever Siri says, your phone doesn't care what you think of it). It's the same for people, the ones who are absorbed by what they do. Whether they're gardeners, baristas, teachers, whatever, it's like they're born to do it and do it to their very best abilities.

This is what you should care about. Focus on this and everything else will be garnish.

But what if you can't shake your other desires?

Then you'll never be free. You'll endlessly be subject to others' vacuous praise, empty wants and petty jealousy. It'll haunt you. You'll always be looking for who will take your stuff, who will trigger your fears, who can be blamed for your misfortunes.

But focus on the core and you'll find peace within. You'll be at one with others around you. You'll be able to roll with whatever happens.

17. ROUGH AND TUMBLE

The elements around us swirl and tumble like a hipster's vape on a windy day. But real virtue is different. It's purposeful, serene and moves in ways we struggle to measure.

18. DON'T FEED THE TROLLS

I tell you, some people, eh? They haven't a good word for those around them but they throw a hissy fit if they aren't praised themselves. They want fame from everyone, even future generations they will never live to see. They might as well moan about not getting any likes from the dead.

19. NO ONE LIKES A QUITTER

Just because something is hard, don't believe it to be impossible. Instead, if it is at all possible, assume *you* can do it.

20. CROSS-TRAINERS CAN BE A BITCH

Say that someone bumps into you in the gym. I bet you wouldn't take offence or think they are out to get you. You wouldn't go and bump them back would you?

You might give them a bit more space – some people are pretty clumsy. But you'd do it good-naturedly. So why not take this and apply it to all areas of your life? If people offend you, give them space and keep your cool.

21. AM I WRONG? GOOD.

If you can prove me wrong, I'll gladly change what I think and do. You see, I want the truth and the truth never hurt anyone. In fact, it's only hanging on to ignorance that does harm.

22. NO OBSTACLES. NONE.

I'll do my thing and let nothing get in the way – doesn't matter if that's people, things or irrational thoughts.

23. BEING REASONABLE

As a human being with reason, be reasonable to the animals and things around you. Treat other reasonable people as brothers and sisters. Stop and think when you need to get things clear in your head. Take your time, there's no rush.

24. MAINLY CARBON

In death, Leonardo da Vinci met the same end as the unknown apprentice that mixed his paints. Either they both went back to the mystical source of all things (if you believe that kind of thing) or they both simply dispersed into atoms.

25. MAN THAT'S BIG

Think about just how much is going on inside every one of us right now and it won't surprise you to learn that there's an almost infinite number of things happening at this very instant right across the universe.

26. SPELL WHAT?

Say someone asks you to spell *'rhythm'*. Would you shout each letter at the top of your voice? And if that angered, would you get angry in return? Or would you speak the letters quietly, one by one?

It's the same with pretty much everything else you do. Things get done in steps. It's down to you to follow those steps without getting wound up with anyone or anything that gets in your way.

Just keep on keeping on.

27. WRONG, WRONG, WRONG

It can be pretty shitty stopping others doing what they think is best for them. But that's what you do when you get all upset with them for doing something you think is wrong. After all, your 'wrong' is their 'right'.

'But they really are wrong!' you cry. OK, then help them see where their real best interests lie rather than just getting wound up about it.

28. CRY FREEDOM
Death is freedom. Freedom from the stuff our senses make up. Freedom from kneejerk subservience to whims and wants. Freedom from the stuff going round and round in our heads. And freedom from being slaves to desire.

29. JUST. ONE. MORE.
Don't let the brain give up when the body can still go on.

30. THIS. ABSOLUTELY THIS.
Don't get drunk on your own power and sense of self-importance. Be good, genuine and unassuming. Be just (and a friend to justice). Be kind – serve the human race and focus always on doing the right thing. Be the person this philosophy would have you be.

Life's short. The only good you can get out of it is to be disciplined on the inside and selfless on the outside.

Get this right and you'll never get tired of being reasonable, moderate and calm. You'll be as indifferent to praise as you'll be to those who would try to bring you down. You'll never give up, never abandon a task, never act in haste. Gossip just won't matter – you'll judge people on their actions and characters, not on some Twitter troll's latest shitstorm. You'll be free of anxiety, naturally brave, not pussyfooting around the things that matter.

More than this, you'll be able to live with little and not regret it for a moment. You'll be fine with hard work because you'll know you're doing the right thing. And you'll be patient because the universe demands it.

You'll be a good and true friend. But you'll speak your mind, disagree when others are wrong and be happy to change your views when others are right. And when death comes calling, you'll head off without worry or regret.

31. SLEEPY TIME IS OVER
Wake up dammit! Remember who you are. Those other things troubling you were just dreams. See them for what they really are.

32. WELCOME TO INDIFFERENCE
I'm one part mind, one part body.

My body is indifferent to what goes on around it because it can't make decisions or form opinions.

As for my mind, the only things that aren't indifferent to it are those it can control – and there aren't many of them. In fact, it can only really concern itself with the present moment as it has no control over either the past or the future.

33. OUCH
A pain in your hand is perfectly natural if it came about from doing what a hand's meant to do. In fact, we can broaden this out – no pain is unnatural if you are doing what you should. It's not evil to suffer, it's just life.

34. NOW THAT'S ODD
Criminals, perverts and tyrants enjoy some pretty weird things.

35. A LINE IN THE SAND
People who know their stuff may try to accommodate the wishes of a less-skilled boss up to a point. But when push comes to shove, they'll draw the line and go no further. It's a matter of principle. Isn't it a shame that the same can't be said for most people who buckle at the first sign of resistance?

36. WHEN YOU LOOK AT IT LIKE THAT
When seen from the perspective of the wider universe, continents are just small corners of dirt, oceans just a drop of water, and Everest a tiny hill of rock.

All the years of our history are just the blink of an eye. Everything in this life of ours is inconsequential and short-lived. And everything comes ultimately from an orderly universe governed by rational laws.

From a lion's gaping jaws to a snake's poison to every last thing that could hurt you, don't think for a second they're not a natural part of the universe.

37. OMNISCIENCE FOR BEGINNERS
To see the present is to see everything that's been before and everything that's yet to come because everything is linked.

38. THINK ABOUT IT
Stop for a while and consider just how interconnected everything is. Everything is interwoven, spooning like long-time lovers, the result of an eternity of obedience to the laws of nature.

39. LIFE IN THE SANDPIT

Be at one with the universe around you. Love others unconditionally. Play nice.

40. DON'T FIGHT IT

It doesn't matter if the person who makes a tool isn't around when it gets used, it'll work anyway. It's different for things in the natural world because nature is still within them. You're no exception. You can't escape the natural laws that govern your being. But work with them and everything will be cool.

41. A BAD IDEA

If you reckon that things outside your control are either good or bad, then when bad stuff happens, chances are you'll go looking for someone or something to blame. But that's a direct route to injustice.

Instead, if you limit what you think of as good or bad just to what's within your own control, there'll be no need to go picking a fight with others.

42. PICK A SIDE

We're all trying to build a better world, even if we don't know it or disagree about what a better world would look like. Everyone plays a part (even the moaners and groaners).

You need to consider what your role in all this will be – whose side are you on? But know this, while whatever you do will have to be in keeping with the wider universe, you should ensure your part is not just a walk-on.

43. DOING THEIR BIT
Does the sun try to do the rain's job? What about the rest of the stars? They may all be different but they're all acting as part of the universe.

44. SO, ABOUT GODS…
Just say there is a god (or a bunch of gods for that matter).

If they spent time plotting my fate, they did a pretty good job. From where I stand, it'd be hard to imagine they have it in for me. And why would they? What would be in it for them? How would it help the wider universe which, you have to think, is their main concern?

OK, even if they don't care a jot about me, I guess I ought to think well of them and anything that happens as a result.

Of course, if they don't care about anything at all, then let's forget the whole prayer and worship thing. Because if this is the case, I'm still able to look after myself and stay true to who I am.

I'm rational. I have a city and a country. As Marcus, I have Rome. And as a human being, I have the world. So whatever is good for these, is good for me.

45. ALL GOOD
As a general rule, what is truly good for one person is good for everyone. We just need to be clear that by good, we mean the stuff that helps real people in the real world rather than any purely moral assessment.

46. SAME, SAME, SAME

Look at your newsfeed – what's really new? It just the same stuff over and over.

It's the same with life as a whole – ups and downs, causes and effects. When will it end?

47. I SEE DEAD PEOPLE

Think about everyone who's ever died – millions and billions of them. Rich, poor, smart, dumb. It's a long list on which your name will appear soon enough – alongside princes and presidents, philosophers and footballers, beauties and bullies.

Think about them all. What did they hope to achieve from life? In reality, the only value lies in seeking truth and being fair (even to those who don't deserve it).

48. CELEBRATE THE AWESOME

When your spirits need a lift, take a moment to think about all the good qualities of your friends – their energy, generosity, modesty, whatever. Nothing is more inspiring to keep in mind.

49. LEAN TIMES

Think yourself too skinny? Would you like to be fatter? How about an extra 150kg? Probably not. So why worry about how much longer you might live? Be happy with what you've got.

50. WE TRY HARDER

Sure, try to get others on your side but, when push comes to shove, act anyway if it's the right thing to do. If they try to stand in your way, stay calm, take a different tack – turn the obstacle into an opportunity to exercise patience and self-control.

Don't forget, you might be wrong and to do the impossible is, well, impossible. It's enough to try your hardest – that is success.

51. DOING HAPPY

Ambitious people tend to find happiness in what others think.

Those who crave pleasure focus on how they feel.

Wise people find it in what they do.

52. OPINIONS ARE LIKE ARSEHOLES…

You don't have to have an opinion. You don't have to get stressed out about things you can't control. These things are not asking for your judgement.

53. BECOMING A MIND READER

Learn how to pay real attention to what people around you are saying. Try to get inside their heads.

54. BEES?

What's useless for the hive is useless for the bee.

55. MAKE CLEVER CHOICES

Want to ignore 'so-called experts'? Who are you going to listen to instead? And will their advice solve anything in the real world?

56. CHECKING OUT

You share the date of your birth with around 300,000 others. Think how many of them have already died.

57. SICK THINKING

If you have jaundice, even honey will taste bitter. Rabies will make you crazily afraid of water. So why do I get angry? Do you think that errors in thinking have any less effect on us than bile or bacteria?

58. LIVE YOUR TRUTH

Nothing can stop you living according to the laws of your personal nature. And nothing can happen that goes against the laws of the universe.

59. I'LL NEVER FORGET WHATSHISNAME

It's sad that we try so hard to please others. To what end?

Yet time will soon wipe it all away. Just think how much you've already forgotten.

THE SEVENTH BOOK

> *'So do you spend a fortune on vitamins and supplements to try to live forever? Or do you run harder in death's shadow without complaint?'*

1. LOOK ON THE FACE OF EVIL
What is evil?

Think about it – whether you look in the news, on your social feeds or in the pages of history, you've seen it all before. From madmen with automatic weapons in schools to Nazis with gas chambers in Poland to Catholic zealots with a thing against 'witches', nothing is new.

The same scenes will be re-enacted in different ways at different times to different degrees. It's as pedestrian as it is pathetic.

2. REMEMBER YOUR FIRST TIME?
Principles die when the circumstances that lead to them are forgotten.

So make sure you keep reminding yourself of why you hold certain things to be true and right. It means you'll be able to quickly make the correct call about what's going on around you, however new it seems.

And if you can't bring the right principle into focus, why worry? It's probably nothing to concern yourself over.

Understand this and you'll have nothing to fear. Simply view events through your previous experience and it'll be like you're born again.

3. THIS IS LIFE

Another must-see show on TV. A dog-whistle tweet. Taking offence. Mock outrage. Trigger warnings. Work. Sleep. Work. Sleep. That's life my friend. And it's your job to take your place among it all – with good humour and without being a dick. Because at the end of the day, you're no more than the things you care about.

4. TALK IS CHEAP

People talk a lot. Some also do stuff. Pay attention to both. For the latter, make sure you understand their purpose. For the former, spend time getting to grips with what they really mean.

5. ARE YOU UP FOR IT?

Are you really up to the task? If so, you should use your mind as nature intended. If not, you should either leave it to someone who knows what they're doing or else find someone to help and simply do your best.

Whichever route you go, one thing is key: to do the right thing to benefit the world around you.

6. GONE. GONE. GONE.

How many once praised 'heroes' are now consigned to oblivion? And how many of those who heaped praise on them are no more too?

7. ASK A COMRADE
It's no big thing to ask for help. Be like a soldier hurling yourself into the breach. You may be hurting, you may not be as fast as you'd like, but you can always find a comrade to help.

8. I LOVE YOU TOMORROW
Never fear the future. No matter what, you'll face it with the same reason and resources that arm you for the present.

9. UNITY FOR BEGINNERS
Everything is connected, woven together – nothing is truly isolated. Together, it all forms a beautiful tapestry, one universe. The multitude makes the whole – all the interplay of natural rules, human laws, reason, logic and truth. And all creatures within can play their part.

10. THE WHOLE IN PART
Every atom is quickly absorbed into the universe. Every cause is soon enveloped by reason. And memories are swiftly buried in the span of eternity.

11. NATURAL IS AS NATURAL DOES
If you're going to be rational about life, any natural act is also a reasonable one.

12. CHOOSE TO ACT
You can either do things or have things done to you.

13. OUT ON A LIMB

Everything that has reason is related, like the parts of a body. They're meant to cooperate to get things done.

You'll understand this better if you see yourself as a limb on a single rational being rather than just a part of the whole. Mere parts get no support from the heart and no pleasure in supporting the whole.

Doing good is therefore a duty to others more than it is an act of self-service.

14. LEAVE VICTIMHOOD BEHIND

For those buffeted by external events, so be it – they'll find plenty to moan about.

Me? I refuse to view whatever happens as evil, and nothing can force me to do otherwise.

15. BE GREEN

Whatever the world says or thinks, I must be good. It's like an emerald saying, *'Whatever the world says, I must be an emerald and keep my colour true.'*

16. BOO!

My mind has no need to create trouble or flights of fancy to seduce or scare. If someone or something else can frighten me, let them go for it. But I won't let my own assumptions help in the effort.

I'll try to avoid physical pain of course and if my body hurts, it'll let me know. But fear and pain only really exist in the mind, so they can only be truly experienced if the mind wills it.

17. UNWELCOME GUESTS

Happiness is about having a good mind, powered by reason. It's a kind of inner god.

So what's this I see? Fantasy? Mental chatter? Idle brain farts? Get out of here, you're not welcome.

I know it's just habit and, don't worry, I'm not angry with you, but get lost.

18. CH-CH-CHANGES

We tend to fear change. But in truth, nothing happens without it. What could be more natural? Could you have a nice hot shower unless the water changed? Could you get energy from food unless your body changed it? Actually, can anything useful happen without change?

It's the same when we die, it's just another change so that our atoms can feed the universe.

19. FEEL THE RUSH

We live our lives like we're in the middle of a fast-moving stream, everything tumbling together, all sharing the same core nature.

Think of how many Einsteins, Bowies and Mandelas have already been swept away. Whoever you are, whatever you do, it's all the same – fast, brief and over too soon.

20. COUNTING SHEEP

The one thing that keeps me awake at night is the thought that I might do something my true self wouldn't agree with or might want done differently or is not ready to do yet.

21. REMEMBER THIS

Soon you'll forget everything and everything will forget you.

22. LIVE AND FORGIVE

At the end of the day, you are perfectly capable of loving those who are dicks towards you. You just have to remember, they are your brothers and sisters. They either don't mean it or are just being dumb. Soon we'll all be dead, and as long as your core being isn't damaged, you haven't really been hurt.

23. WHAT'S NEXT?

The universe is endlessly making and remaking stuff out of the same atoms. First it's a tree, then a dung beetle, then an iPhone, then you and then something else entirely.

Each of these exists for the briefest time. So why should the destruction of these things be any more threatening than their making?

24. GRRR

Angry faces aren't natural. The more you slap a scowl on your visage, the less beautiful you'll look (inside and out). Keep it up and, in the end, there'll be no coming back.

It's the same with reason – when it's gone, it's super-difficult to regain.

25. BORN AGAIN
Everything around you will soon become something else. Soon after, that too will be transformed into something even newer. And on and on. It keeps the world young.

26. PEOPLE JUST LIKE YOU?
When somebody is an arse towards you, ask yourself, *'What were they thinking?'*

Once you understand that, chances are your anger will turn into pity. If they acted as you would have, you'll probably forgive them (after all, you'd have done the same). If you've managed to get beyond artificial ideas of good and evil, it'll be easier to tolerate others who aren't there yet.

27. IT'S JUST STUFF
Don't lust after stuff you don't have or you'll be a slave to your wants and desires. Instead, think about the things you already own that bring you the most joy. Imagine how much you'd want them if you didn't already own them. But be careful, don't fixate on them so much that you'd flip out if you were to lose them tomorrow.

28. SANCTUARY
Your inner self is your sanctuary. Knowing that you did the right thing is all you will ever need to be at peace.

29. DREAM NO MORE

Ditch the daydreams. Stop being a slave to the *what ifs* and *wouldn't it be nices*.

Focus on the here and now. Learn to see what's really happening (whether to you or to others). Break things down into what's really causing them. Think about your final hour on Earth and leave others' wrongs with them.

30. FOCUS. FOCUS. FOCUS.

Focus on what people are really saying. Go deep into what's happening and who's doing it.

31. TWO LAWS

Let others see your simplicity, self-respect and indifference (whether to the good or the bad). Love your fellow humans. Remember, there are only two laws that pretty much govern everything we do: physical laws and moral laws. That should be enough for anyone.

32. THE BIG D

So, about death… If you think about the entire universe simply being made up of atoms, death is just dispersion. Of course, if you think about it as a unified whole, death is simply metamorphosis.

33. OUCHY, OUCH, OUCH

So, about pain… If pain is really unbearable, it'll kill you. Anything else is bearable.

You can stay calm by distancing your mind from the pain. Leave the hurt parts to make their case (if they can).

34. I WANT TO LIVE FOREVER...
So, about fame... Just look at the minds of those who lust after fame. They run from this, they run after that. Just like a beach wiped clean after each high tide, today's fame will be erased by tomorrow's celebrity.

35. A NEW PERSPECTIVE
If you met someone who had true vision across all time and matter, do you think they'd care much about the life of a single person? No.

And would they be scared of death? No way.

36. GOOD DEEDS PUNISHED
It's the fate of great people to be spoken of badly for trying to do good things.

37. LOOK AT YOU
It sucks that your mind can make your face do whatever it likes but can't have the same power over its own thoughts.

38. STUFF AND NONSENSE
Don't worry about stuff – it sure as hell doesn't worry about you.

39. BRINGING THE HAPPY
Whether you're focused on immortal gods or the rest of us doomed to die, bring joy.

40. AND IN YOUR PRIME TOO
Like long grass in the face of a Flymo, some are cut down while others survive.

41. CARE NOT
If the universe doesn't care about me and those I love, there has to be a reason.

42. POWERFUL ALLIES
At the end of the day, I have right and justice on my side.

43. NOT IN MY GANG
I'll not be joining those that cry or those that fear.

44. EASY DECISIONS
You're wrong if you think anyone worth anything worries about living or dying. They simply decide what to do based on whether it is right and fair or wrong and unjust.

45. THE LAST STAND?
Here's the thing: Wherever you make your stand (whether due to your

judgement or another's influence) that's where you need to face the music – let everything else go screw itself.

46. YOU CAN'T SAVE EVERYONE
Sometimes, doing the right thing may mean going beyond saving yourself or others from harm.

Ultimately, you shouldn't cling to life no matter what. You need to let things happen as they will, embrace your destiny and make the most of the time you have.

47. THE FINAL FRONTIER?
Look up at the stars. You're already travelling among them. Let this thought free you from the tedious parts of life on Earth.

48. LOOK DOWN
According to Plato (and a whole bunch of people who've been up to space), anyone who wants to make pronouncements about the world should look down on events from way up above.

Peace. War. Love. Hate. Births. Deaths. Family. Foreigners. People of every kind doing every kind of thing.

From this vantage point, it's all one crazy harmonious mix.

49. THE PAST IS THE FUTURE
Look at history and you'll see the future. It repeats over and over, both different and the same. Study people for a year, a century, millennia and

it's all the same. What else do you expect?

50. THE RETURN TICKET
Everything created on Earth will return to it. Everything made of stardust will revert to it. Or to put it another way, everything returns to the simple atoms that make it.

51. SMILE BACK
Do you spend a fortune on vitamins and supplements to try to live forever? Or do you run harder in death's shadow without complaint?

52. IT'S NOT ABOUT WINNING
Some people might be faster to get one over on others, but they won't be more public-spirited, humble and ready to roll with the punches, forgiving those who put them down.

53. NEVER FEAR DOING THE RIGHT THING
When you can do good using the same reason we share with the wisest among us, you need fear nothing. When you stay true and do the right thing, you'll not be harmed.

54. I HAVE THE POWER
You always have the power to be happy with what you've got, to be fair to others and to watch out for crazy thoughts that could mess up your head.

55. IT'S YOUR MIND
Don't look to others to tell you what to do, trust your own thinking and values, and do what needs to be done.

Everyone must do what's right as they see it. You can't concern yourself with every fool, nutjob and troll you encounter. Instead, look to other rational people as brothers and sisters.

Don't be swayed by empty wants and desires – the grumbling belly, the stirring in your pants. These are just baseless instincts that want to rule your life.

Stay strong. It's your mind that controls your body, not the other way around. Finally, don't give in to being rushed or hoodwinked, let your mind plot a more enlightened course.

56. DIED (AND GOT BETTER)
Take a second to imagine you've just died and by some kind of miracle, you've been given a new life. Live it to the full in harmony with the world around you.

57. LOVING LIFE
Love your life – every part that makes up your destiny – but nothing more. After all, what else do you really need?

58. NEVER LIKED SNOWFLAKES
Whenever things go wrong, think about all those snowflakes who reacted with wailing, hissy fits and #IT'S_SO_UNFAIRs.

What did it do for them? Nothing. Zilch. Nada.

Do you want the same to happen to you? Leave these reactions to others and focus on turning whatever happened into something useful – a valuable opportunity to build your resilience.

Whatever happens, whatever you do is down to you and you alone. The crisis in question? It's of little consequence.

59. DIG FOR VICTORY
Look deep inside. That's where you'll find your essential goodness. Keep digging and you'll keep finding it.

60. SIT UP DAMMIT!
Whether you're standing or sitting, don't slouch. Just as you can tell a lot about someone from their expression, the same is true of the rest of the body. But make it natural, no faking.

61. PUT 'EM UP
Life is more like a fight than a dance. You need to stay on your feet without panicking, even while you're being pushed and hit from every side – sometimes from places and foes you'd never expect.

62. LIKE TO BE LIKED?
Make sure you get to know the people who you really wish liked you. Figure out what truly drives them. Why do they think and act the way they do?

That way you won't get bent out of shape if they don't say good things about you – in fact, you won't care much either way.

63. BE GENTLE WITH ME
The philosopher Plato once said, *'No one wilfully abandons the truth.'*

It's the same for justice, wisdom, kindness and all the other virtues. Remember this and you'll treat others with the gentleness they deserve.

64. PAIN AND THE LIKE
Whenever you're hurting, remember this: There's nothing shameful about pain, and pain can't affect your mind unless you let it.

The philosopher Epicurus had it right: *'Pain is never unbearable or unending as long as you know its limits and don't imagine it's worse than it is.'*

And it's not just pain. The same is true of tiredness, illness and heartbreak. Whenever you fall victim to anything like this, remind yourself, *'I'm giving in to pain.'*

65. HATERS GONNA HATE
Don't make the mistake of feeling for haters and trolls what they feel for others.

66. REBEL WITH A CAUSE?
How do we know that James Dean was not a better person than Marilyn Monroe? It proves nothing to compare their careers, how they delivered a line, who they slept with or how they died. None of that really matters.

What does matter is what were they like on the inside? Did they treat others with compassion and fairness? Did they allow others to adversely influence them?

Ultimately, did they do the right thing when it mattered without being knocked off course by idle fears, dreams and fancies?

67. MAKE THE MOST OF WHAT YOU HAVE

The mind and body are not so bound up that the mind doesn't know where it ends and everything else begins. It is perfectly capable of remaining separate.

Don't forget that you need very little to be truly happy. Sure, you may not be the next Einstein, da Vinci or Mozart, but you can still be free in your own thoughts and generous to those around you. You can still live up to your full potential even if others never see it.

68. IT'S ALL USEFUL

Live freely and calmly even if it seems everyone around you is hell-bent on being total arses.

No matter what, there's nothing stopping your mind from remaining untroubled, making correct judgements about events and capturing every opportunity that comes your way.

Get this right and your mind will happily assert, *'This is the truth, no matter what others say.'* And when opportunities turn up, you'll be able to greet them with, *'So there you are, I was just looking for you.'*

Whatever happens, every event offers you the chance to be more human and more rational. Everything, good or bad, is useful. Nothing is ever really unsolvable or beyond our imagination – it's all familiar and helpful.

69. MAYBE TODAY?
To live each day as if it was your last, without rushing or dawdling or living in denial, that's the perfection of character.

70. THE UNIVERSE HAS A POINT
You don't hear the universe grumbling about all the crap it has to put up with, it just goes on providing the perfect environment for us to thrive in (when, that is, we're not screwing it up).

So how can you, who'll be gone in the blink of a cosmic eye, complain about being tired or bored or whatever? Doesn't that make you kind of pathetic?

71. OUT OF MY HANDS
Isn't it crazy that I don't make the effort to avoid harming other people, which is easy enough, yet do everything I can to avoid being harmed by others who I simply can't control?

72. DUMB JUDGEMENT
If you think something is stupid or unfriendly, you can happily judge it as inferior. No problem.

73. NO CHEERS, NO APPLAUSE
When you've done a good deed and someone else has benefited, shouldn't

that be reward enough? Why do you need anything more? It's only idiots who are desperate for prizes and applause.

74. YOUR JUST DESSERTS

OK, I know, no one ever gets sick of receiving a reward. Who doesn't enjoy a bit of external validation? But doing the right thing is a reward in its own right. So never get tired of helping others as this is a direct route to rewarding yourself.

75. IT'S SIMPLY LOGICAL, CAPTAIN

After the Big Bang went off, everything else that happened was simply a logical next step. If this wasn't the case, nothing would make sense. Remember this and you'll be way more chill about everything.

THE EIGHTH BOOK

> 'Win with modesty. Lose with grace.'

1. A DOSE OF REALITY
OK, reality check time.

There's no way you can claim to have fully lived up to your potential as someone who uses reason in all things and always does the right thing. Even if we ignore childhood ignorance and those awkward years around puberty, such a claim just won't stand up to the slightest challenge.

Your mind is likely to have been regularly confused and chances are, this will continue. Your whole life – who you are, what you do, who you hang out with – all provide ample opportunity for negative influences. This is just the way it is.

The good news is, once you wise up to this, you should no longer give an actual shit about how others see you. All you can do is try your best to be true to yourself and true to what nature would have you be from now on. Understand what this means and refuse to become distracted by all the noise around you.

Before today, all your attempts at discovering the good life are likely to have been unsuccessful. You haven't found it in clever thinking, money, celebrity, sex, drugs or rock and roll.

So where is it? In doing the right thing.

Be hard on yourself. Don't slack or make excuses. Determine what's right and what's wrong. Understand that nothing is right that doesn't help you be fair, self-disciplined, courageous and free.

2. A QUICK QUESTION

Before you do anything, ask yourself: *What will be the consequences of this? Is this something I'm going to regret? All too soon I'll be dead and forgotten, but until then, is what I'm about to do right in the eyes of my fellow humans and common morality?*

3. AN UNFAIR COMPARISON?

Winston Churchill, Lenin, JFK – who are they compared to Socrates, Einstein and Stephen Hawking?

The latter looked deep into the true nature of the world. They shared a common drive, stayed true to reason. The others? Yes, they were responsible for momentous events but they were also enslaved by petty things too.

4. THROWING YOUR TOYS OUT OF THE PRAM

Sure, you may explode in some screaming tantrum but others will simply get on with getting on.

5. SIMPLE

Don't worry. Seriously, don't. Everything is bound to the laws of nature and soon enough, you'll be a distant memory.

So focus on what you've got to do right now. Split reality from fantasy. Do your best. Be good. Stick to the path of an honest, just person. Be kind. That's it.

6. THE RESTLESS WORLD
The universe is continually moving stuff around, transforming it into this and that. Change is everywhere but there's nothing to be afraid of. It's all predictable and entirely natural.

7. FOLLOW YOUR PATH
Everyone's core nature is content following its own path. If your nature is governed by reason, this will mean avoiding the false and fake, focusing on the common good, ignoring things that are outside your reach and rolling with the punches.

Your core nature is a part of the wider universe in the same way a leaf is part of a tree. But a leaf has no reason, feels nothing and doesn't get upset if someone trolls it on Twitter.

Human nature, however, is part of a universal nature which is free, mindful and fair. It's what gives us our share of time, resources and the world around us – maybe not equally from individual to individual but in the wider environment.

8. TODAY'S LESSON
'School's out, I've nothing left to learn,' you might say.

Well you can learn to watch against arrogance.

You can learn to rise above pleasure and pain.

You can learn not to worry whether you're popular or well-liked.

And you can learn not to be upset by friends and foes alike (and even to care for them in spite of everything).

9. NOT ANOTHER WORD
No one should ever hear you moaning about your life (not even you).

10. FOMO
You'll tend to regret missed opportunities.

Now, of course, anything good is useful and something people care about. But no one should regret missing out on pleasure. Pleasure in itself is neither good nor useful.

11. PROBING QUESTIONS
When you see anything, ask: *What is this really? What's it made of? What's its true function? How long will it last?*

12. SLEEPY?
When you're feeling sleepy and can't be bothered, remember that doing the right thing for others is part of human nature. Sleep, however, you share with warthogs and dung beetles. Ultimately, keeping faith with your higher nature is always going to be more satisfying and fulfilling.

13. PROVE IT
Always test your thinking against the facts. Does it really hold up?

14 IS THIS PERSON A DICK?
Whenever you meet someone, immediately ask yourself, *'What do they believe is good and evil, right and wrong?'* Because once you get that straight, you'll never be surprised to find their actions stay true to form. They have no choice.

15. NO SURPRISES
Are you surprised that an apple tree bears apples? Then why be surprised when the wider world bears its own crop of events?

It's like a doctor being surprised to meet a patient with a funny-looking rash.

Or a cab driver being surprised that someone might want to be driven somewhere.

16. SO, YOU'RE WRONG
At the end of the day, it's no limit to your freedom to change your mind when someone shows you that you're wrong. After all, it's your reason and judgement that allow you to accept that change is possible in the first place.

17. THE BLAME GAME
If it's your decision, why do it? If it's another's decision, who are you going to blame? God? Atoms? Either would be crazy and pointless.

If someone gets something wrong, try to correct them. If that's not possible, correct what they did. And if you can't do that, why bother with blame? It's just not worth it.

18. REMAINS

When something dies, it doesn't vanish from the universe. It's still here. It just changes into its constituent atoms. The same atoms that make up everything in the universe. And you don't hear them bitching about change.

19. WHAT'S YOUR ROLE?

Everything, from bananas to baboons, exists for a reason. Even the sun has a job to do.

So why are you here? Simply for pleasure? The mere thought is pathetic.

20. BEGINNING, MIDDLE AND END

Nature rules the beginning, middle and end of all things.

It's like someone throwing a Frisbee. Does the disc benefit on the way up? Is it hurt by its descent? Or even as it rolls off down the beach? How does a bubble benefit from holding itself together instead of bursting?

It's all part of the whole.

21. TAKE YOUR CLOTHES OFF

Get naked. Take a good look at yourself – check out the signs of age, illness, heavy nights spent partying.

Life is just as short for those who praise others as for those on the receiving end of praise. Same for those who remember others and who are themselves remembered after their time.

And even if this time is short, confined to some grotty little hellhole, the entirety of everything on Earth is just a tiny blue dot in the vastness of the universe.

22. PAY ATTENTION
Do what needs doing right now with your whole attention – whether you're focused on an object, an activity, a principle or what someone is saying.

Of course, you're going to be disappointed if you'd prefer to hope for goodness tomorrow rather than getting on with being good today.

23. DO OR BE DONE
If I'm going to do something, I want it to be for the good of the human race. If I'm on the receiving end, I'll accept it as just a part of the greater tapestry of the universe.

24. PASS THE SOAP
Think of your bath just after you've got out. A soup of oil, sweat and dirt. Pretty grim really. But all of life is like this, as is everything within it.

25. EXTINCTION AGAIN
We all die.

When I pass, my children will bury me. In time, their children will bury them or see them go up in smoke. It's always been this way.

Thousands of years of smart people, arrogant people, downright odd people – where are they now? All those geniuses, gone in a flash, some forgotten, some remembered as heroes and legends.

So think about how your wonderful, complex body will one day be broken down into its atoms and scattered. Your little life extinguished and everything that makes up your body recycled by the universe.

26. TRUE HAPPINESS

Want to love what you do? Be true to your calling. Love others. Don't trust your senses. Work out what's true and false for yourself. Understand the universe as best you can.

27. THREE RELATIONSHIPS

We all have three relationships. The first is with our bodies. The second is with our fellow humans. The third is with the wider universe around us.

28. IMAGINARY PAIN

Pain can be bad for the body or bad for the mind.

If it's the body, let it complain how it likes. If it's the mind, well, the mind has a say in this. It can simply refuse to play and remain calm and untroubled instead.

You see, it's ultimately up to the mind whether it is affected by every trouble, slight, desire and petty abuse that comes its way. None of this can trouble the mind without its consent.

29. FREE YOUR MIND
Be free from mental turmoil by repeating to yourself, *'It's up to me whether I allow stupidity, anger, desire and all the rest of it in. I can see things as they really are and decide their worth.'*

Remember, this ability is nature's gift to you.

30. YOUR NEXT SPEECH
Whether speaking to princes and presidents or to beggars and bloggers, use language that's reasonable but true to who you are. Say it straight. Say it true.

31. LAST ONE STANDING
Look at the court of Queen Victoria. Her husband. Her nine children. Her friends. Her ancestors. Everyone she ever met.

All dead.

Think about the deaths of others, not just individuals, whole bloodlines. Go to one of the old-world cathedrals or abbeys, you'll see plenty of engravings that proclaim, *'Last of his line'*.

Despite all the attempts to produce heirs, someone had to be last, and another line exited this universe.

32. NONSTOP FULFILMENT
Everything you do should contribute to a fulfilling life.

If you manage this, be happy. After all, this is something no one else can prevent.

'*But others will try to influence me,*' you might say.

They can try, but they can't stop you living in accordance with fairness, wisdom and reason.

'*But what if they physically stop me?*' you could ask.

Maybe. But not if you roll with it and adapt your approach while still remaining true to your ultimate course.

33. EITHER WAY
Win with modesty. Lose with grace.

34. A TRIAL SEPARATION
Have you ever seen a severed hand or foot? Or even a head? Even if you haven't, you can probably imagine it.

Well, this is what people do to themselves when they refuse to accept reality or live in denial or selfishly stand alone. They become outcasts from the natural world (even though they were born into it). They become cut off.

But here's a lovely thought: Even if this is you, you can still become reunited.

This makes humans pretty special in the universe. Not only are you a part of the natural world, even if you become separated, you can still find your way back.

35. IT'S ALL NATURAL
As part of the natural world, you have all the powers that all animals share. Just as nature absorbs all creatures into the whole, you too can absorb every hindrance and obstacle into something you can use for your own ends.

36. IT'S JUST NOW
Don't freak yourself out imagining the entirety of your life. Don't dwell on everything that could happen, all the troubles and pain that may come your way. Instead, take each day as it comes and ask, *'What's so unendurable here?'*

You'll discover your answer may be a bit embarrassing.

Then remember, it's not the weight of the future or the past that's pressing down on you. It's always the present that really counts.

When you look at it like this, problems become small things. In fact, when you refuse to let things get out of proportion, chances are, you'll cope just fine.

37. LET THE DEAD BE DEAD
Should I stay mourning by my grandmother's grave? If I did, would she know? And if she knew, would she be happy about it?

If she was happy, could I expect to go on living forever? Am I not destined to become old and die one day? And what would my grandmother do then? It's all just a sackful of stench and rot.

38. WELL LOOK AT THAT
If you've got a pair of functioning eyes, use them. See things for what they really are.

39. IT'S IN YOUR NATURE
In a rational person you'll see no natural ability that runs counter to justice. But you will find an abundance of self-control to counter empty pleasures.

40. IMAGINARY PAIN
Forget what you simply imagine to be painful and it'll be impossible to harm you.

'But my mind isn't all that I am,' you might say.

True. Then refuse to let your mind be hurt and leave the rest of your body to keep its pain to itself.

41. IMPERVIOUS CLARITY
Anything that hinders our senses or actions is fundamentally bad for our core being.

It's the same with the mind where anything that hinders clear thinking will be a burden on its core nature.

Apply this to your situation. Do you feel pain or pleasure? Your senses will tell you.

Have your plans been screwed over? Well, if you got all *'I simply must have this'* about it, then sure, that sucks.

But what did you expect? You failed to see the world clearly.

If you make sure your desires are within the limits of reason, these issues will simply vanish. That's because nothing and no one can frustrate the mind.

Not fire and fury.

Not Facebook and Twitter trolls.

In fact, nothing whatsoever.

42. PLAY NICE WITH YOURSELF
If I've never intentionally harmed another person, what right have I to harm myself?

43. THINGS I LOVE
People like all sorts of stuff. Me? I love clarity of thought. I love standing up and being counted in this crazy world we live in. I love being able to look at the world around me, with all its faults, and view it with good spirit. I love giving everyone their fair dues.

44. ENTERING NOW. POPULATION: YOU
Luxuriate in the present. Those who chase the future forget that the people whose respect they so desire will be just the same as those they think of as arses today.

What's more, they'll all soon be dead anyway. So what do you care?

45. CALM LIKE YODA
Do what you like with me, my inner self will remain calm as long as I'm true to who I am.

Is a simple change in circumstances enough to upset me?

Will it make me hide under the blanket and gorge on ice cream?

Could anything be enough to do this?

46. NOTHING'S UNNATURAL
Nothing can happen to you that's unnatural. Same as nothing unnatural can happen to a plant or a dog or a pebble.

So what's there to bitch about when all these others put up with what's natural to them? This same nature won't hit you with anything you can't endure.

47. GETTING STUFF DONE
If something is getting to you, the pain you're feeling isn't due to the thing itself, it's down to how you perceive it.

You have the power to change this whenever you like. If the pain is inside, due to some issue with your character, then what's stopping you from fixing it?

And if it is down to worrying about something you have to do, why not use the energy you're wasting to simply get on with it?

'But there's this huge, unstoppable thing in the way!' you cry.

OK, don't worry then. If that's really the case and you can't get around it, it's not your fault. Get on with other things.

'But I have to get it done or life just won't be worth living!' you come back.

Really? Well, then you'll be able to slip away free from worry same as anyone who has done all they can.

48. INSIDE YOUR MIND PALACE

You'll realise just how powerful your mind is when it puts up the shutters and decides no way, no how is it going to do something (even when that decision is crazy).

So imagine what it'd be like to have that same strength as a result of deciding calmly and rationally.

Without all the usual wants and desires, the mind can be an absolute fortress. In fact, you couldn't find a better place to protect yourself from the outside world.

If you can't see this, you're being dumb. And if you can see it but don't take advantage, you really are being foolish.

49. KEEP IT REAL
Don't blow things up beyond what your senses tell you is happening.

Say you're told someone has been bad mouthing you. That's it. The message doesn't say it's done you any harm.

Or you might see your child is ill. OK. But you don't see that they are in any real danger.

So stick with your initial impressions. Don't embellish them and add details that simply aren't there. If you're going to add anything, make it that whatever is happening is just a part of the greater way of the universe.

50. MOTHER NATURE IS AN ARTIST
'This milk is off.' Then pour it down the sink.

'There's dog shit on the pavement.' Then walk round it.

'My train is late.' Then either wait or go another way.

That's enough. Don't go on to whine about why these things are brought into the world.

Hearing this, any naturalist would simply laugh at you – in the same way a carpenter or shoemaker would laugh at you if you complained about the sawdust and leather offcuts in their workshops.

Of course, they've got somewhere to throw out their rubbish. Mother Nature, however, is stuck with it. But the beauty of the natural world is its ability to transform matter from one thing into something completely new. Ma Nature wastes nothing, recycles everything and doesn't need a rubbish dump. She just gets on with it, in her own time, with what she has to hand.

51. THE JOY OF WET FEET
Don't be slow to act. Don't ramble or go off on one. Don't vanish up yourself with introspection (or drive people nuts unburdening every emotion). And don't live simply to work.

Just because people may attack you – verbally, physically, mentally – why should this affect your mind's ability to remain calm, sane and fair?

You could stand in a crystal-clear mountain spring and hurl abuse at the water. But it'd still go on flowing. Say you threw mud and shit in it (please don't). It'd soon wash away.

So how can you have your own inner mental spring? By ensuring you stay in control of your mind every second of the day, remaining compassionate, unaffected and modest.

52. TWO THINGS TO UNDERSTAND
If you don't understand the nature of the universe, you'll never find your place within it. And you can't understand the nature of the universe without understanding its purpose. Failure on both counts means you'll never have a good answer for why you're here.

So why worry about seeking the praise of all those who have no idea what's going on and their place within it?

53. JUST NOT WORTH IT

Would you want praise from someone who's always moaning about their life? Do you want to please someone who isn't pleased with themselves? How can anyone be pleased with themselves when they seem to regret almost everything they do?

54. BREATHE IN SOME SMARTS

Just as you breathe in oxygen from the atmosphere, think with the intelligence of the natural world you're part of. This kind of knowledge and understanding is everywhere around you, just like air.

55. YOU'RE ONLY HURTING YOURSELF

Doing wrong won't harm the universe. It won't even really harm the person on the receiving end. The real harm is to the perpetrator and they can stop it anytime they choose.

56. YOU ARE AN ISLAND

What others think is no more important than their breath or flesh. No matter how much we are all fellow humans, every individual has ultimate power over themselves. If this wasn't so, others would have control over us. And no one wants their happiness controlled by another.

57. I'VE SEEN THE LIGHT

The sun does its whole shining thing yet doesn't get used up (and won't for a few billion years). And when you examine the sun's rays, you'll see they'll carry on until they hit some solid object. There they stay without slipping off.

You should view thoughts in the same way. Extending off in a straight line, not expiring, not breaking up when they hit an obstacle but resting there, lighting things up for a better view.

58. DEADLY AFRAID?
If you're afraid of dying, you either fear losing sensation or gaining a new one.

In reality, you'll either feel nothing (in which case, no problem) or if you feel something new, you'll be some new creature (in which case, you didn't really die).

59. RUBBING ALONG
We're all here for one another. So either teach others to be better or shut up and put up.

60. BANG, BANG
A bullet heads in one direction, a thought in another. But with proper aim, even for the most complex problems, a thought heads towards its target just as directly.

61. SHARE YOUR THINKING
Spend time understanding how others think and let them understand how you do too

THE NINTH BOOK

> *'Outside your front door, that's the world. It's what it is, no more, no less. It's not self-aware, it doesn't pass judgement on itself.'*

1. ALL MANNER OF SINS

Acting unfairly is just plain wrong.

Any rational being will help others who deserve it and, certainly, avoid harming them.

The same goes for lying.

Everything in existence is connected to everything that's ever existed. Truth is core to this. A lie is wrong because it is, at heart, an act of injustice. Even an unintentional lie upsets the harmony of the universe. And the more people lie, the less they're able to tell lies from truth.

It's also wrong to seek pleasures as if they're good and avoid pain as if it's evil. We see it all around us – bad people chase after pleasure and the stuff that gives them pleasure while good people suffer pain and hardship.

Besides, anyone afraid of pain is ultimately afraid of something that'll happen to them anyway as part of the natural order of things. This is crazy. It's the same with the fool that doesn't hesitate to do whatever unjust thing gets them closer to the pleasures they lust after.

Ultimately, the universe is indifferent to pain and pleasure. So if we're going to live in harmony with reality, we should be too. Agony and ecstasy. Death and life. Fame and obscurity. It's all the same in the end.

In saying all this, I mean that step follows step, from the Big Bang to the second you read this sentence.

It's all part of an endless chain of cause and effect. And so here we are.

2. TIME TO ESCAPE

Given the choice, most people would prefer to never experience lies, hypocrisy, greed and pride. But as that's not an option, the next best thing is to push them away.

Or are you happy to go on putting up with it all?

Hasn't experience taught you to do everything you can to escape from this plague? The damage it's doing to your mind and inner peace is far deadlier than breathing the air of a polluted city street.

It's not just that it harms our minds, it damages our humanity.

3. WELL HELLO DEATH

Don't be afraid of death. Give it a winning smile and a cheeky wink. It's just another essential part of nature after all. Like being young or growing old, with all its wrinkles, aches and forgetfulness.

The ultimate end is just another event along the way. If you've given it some thought, you won't view death carelessly, impatiently or scornfully. Even as you await the birth of your firstborn child, you should also anticipate the moment you finally depart the world of the living.

But if you need a bit more reassurance, there's no better comfort than to consider the world around you – the people you'll no longer have to put up with, the crap in the attic you'll never have to sort out.

While you should treat others fairly and respectfully in everyday life, ultimately they don't view the world as you do. If the one thing that would have glued you to the mortal world was the desire to hang out with some kindred spirits, all the petty disputes and arguments and one-upping should make you welcome death with open arms and a cheery, *'Let's do this before I forget myself.'*

4. SINNERS
Sinners sin against themselves. But evildoers do evil to themselves by being bad.

5. SINS OF OMISSION
Evil isn't just about what people do, it's often what they don't do that causes the most harm.

6. ENOUGH ALREADY
Everything is good if you're being objective in your thinking, unselfish in your actions and calm in your attitude no matter what's happening.

7. GIVE ROOM TO RATIONALITY
Ditch the fantasy. Curb your impulses. Dampen your desire. Let your mind rule.

8. SHARING IS CARING

Every living creature shares the same life force. All humans share the capability to be rational. And we all share this single planet, with a single sun and a single atmosphere.

9. GRAVITATIONAL PULL

As the saying goes, birds of a feather flock together.

Everything has gravity. Water flows to meet more water. Gases mix and blend. (Only hard barriers or brute force can keep them apart.) Fire leaps skyward and towards anything that burns easily (and which can't therefore resist it).

It's the same with anyone who shares a core spirit of rational thought. They're eager to join with other like-minded people (if anything, this pull is even stronger given their focus).

In the rest of the natural world, bees swarm, cows herd, birds flock. Likewise, rational people hang out with others in cities, coffee shops and clubs. Even in wartime, these are the ones who forge the truces.

This attraction extends all the way up to the stars whose gravitational pull draws them together over vast distances.

Of course, in these crazy times we live in, we see people forget this natural attraction. They drift apart. They disagree. But even as they do, they can never escape, the pull is too strong.

You're more likely to find an atom not of this universe than you are to find someone totally divorced from all of humanity.

10. GIVE ME SOME SUGAR

Everything bears fruit in its own time. It's not just plants, reason also bears fruit, both for itself and the wider world. And man, it tastes sweet.

11. BE KIND, ALWAYS

If you can change people's bad behaviour, do it. If not, remember to be kind.

The universe sometimes conspires to help such people, leading them to better health or greater wealth. So what's preventing you from doing the same?

12. HARD WORK

Work hard. I don't mean like a slave or someone looking for pity but as someone totally committed to doing the right thing.

13. FREE AGAIN

Today, I freed myself from confusion. Well, to be clear, I freed confusion from me. You see, it wasn't outside, it was within and relying on my point of view.

14. NO CHANGE THERE THEN

Every experience is commonplace, short-lived and easily corrupted. It's the same today as it's always been, reaching back to the dawn of time.

15. GET OUT

Outside your front door, that's the world. It's what it is, no more, no less.

It's not self-aware, it doesn't pass judgement on itself.

So how do you judge it? Use your mind.

16. I DON'T CARE HOW YOU FEEL
Good and evil lie in what people do, not how they feel. Just as their behaviour, good and bad, is about what they do.

17. UPS AND DOWNS
To a yo-yo, there's no evil in dropping just as there's no good in rising.

18. EVERYONE'S A CRITIC
If you take time to look inside people's motivations, you'll see the kinds of critics you are so scared of. But you'll also see how rubbish they are at criticising themselves.

19. TRANSFORMERS
Everything changes. You too. Every day, you're in a process of transformation. But so is the universe.

20. LEAVE IT ALONE
When others do wrong, just leave it.

21. MANY DEATHS
When anything stops – an activity, an impulse, an opinion – there's no evil.

Look at the stages of life: babe in arms, childhood, adolescence, adulthood, old age. Each ended in a kind of death. Were they so scary?

Or think about how you lived with your parents or your grandparents or with aunts and uncles but have now moved on. When you look at all these changes, ask yourself, 'Was there anything to be afraid of?'

No. And it's exactly the same with your ultimate death.

22. MIND-READING THE UNIVERSE
Be quick to look into your own mind, your neighbour's mind and the mind of the universe.

Make sure your mind is fair. As for your neighbour, figure out whether they act on purpose or out of ignorance, and never forget, they are a fellow human. And as for the universe, simply remind yourself that you are part of something far bigger than you.

23. COMMUNITY VALUES
You are part of the community around you. So every action should benefit that community. Anything else harms the community as a whole. It's like that guy on Twitter who can't resist trolling everyone around him.

24. YOU COULDN'T MAKE IT UP
Childish arguments and temper tantrums. Petty games of make-believe. Tiny breaths sustaining corpses.

The world of ghosts and fairies is more solid than this.

25. HOW LONG?

Job one: Get to the heart of what's causing events. Split this out from the effects. Study it closely. Then work out how long the root cause can sustain the effects.

26. ENOUGH IS ENOUGH

You are on the receiving end of all sorts of problems simply because you won't let reason guide you. Enough already!

27. CARING, NOT CARING

When people are dicks towards you, look deeply into their hearts. Try to work out what kind of people they really are.

Chances are, you'll quickly see that there's nothing to be gained by making efforts to get into their good graces. All the same, try to view them with kindness. They are fellow humans. They face all the same trials and tribulations you do.

28. CYCLES WITHIN CYCLES

The universe works in cycles. Maybe there is some kind of fate that triggers everything. If so, go with it. Or maybe there actually was some form of master event that started the ball rolling and that everything else is simply a consequence.

Fate or consequences, who cares? Whichever it is, you can't do much about it apart from applying your mind to what to do next.

Pretty soon, we'll all revert to a bunch of atoms. Later, so will the Earth.

Whatever the consequences, change will be inevitable and endless (until time itself ends). To understand all this is to view our little bit of mortality with indifference.

29. KEEPING IT SIMPLE, KEEPING IT REAL
The progress of the universe is like a flood that carries everything else along. How pathetic it is that small people play at politics and imagine they're some gift to the world. Snot-nosed toddlers!

What does it really take to be fully human? Precisely what nature is demanding right now. Right. Now.

No delay. No worrying if anyone is watching. Don't try to boil the ocean, just get started. Small steps. And understand that this is a pretty big deal in its own right.

You're not going to change people's true convictions, and without that, it's all just a façade. The best you can hope for is some grudging obedience or face-saving acceptance.

Go ahead. Tell me all about all the gurus and heroes and wise eggs. If they learned about the will of nature, good for them. But if they were just playing the part, why should I follow their examples?

The good life is a simple one, a modest one. That's what will stop me becoming a pretentious jerk.

30. CRUISING ALTITUDE
Imagine you're in a plane, looking down on the mass of people and all their comings and goings, in good times and bad.

Look at all the fantastic creatures that are born, live with each other and then die. All the long-dead generations before you. All those who haven't been born yet. All those living in some far-flung region of the planet.

How many haven't even heard of you? Or how many have quickly forgotten your name and unsubscribed from your thoughts, posts and updates?

How many are loving your work right now but will be slagging you off in the near future?

Whether it's fame, glory or whatever, it's all ultimately worthless.

31. PAINT A RAINBOW

When you're up against something you can't control, relax. When you do act, always be honest and fair. In either case, focus on making the world a better place for others while being true to yourself.

32. THINK BIGGER, THINK WIDER

A lot of the stuff that winds you up can easily be got rid of. The reality is, it's all in your head. You can always think bigger, expanding your mind to focus on the wider universe or the eternity of existence or on how everything is always changing.

Think of the brief span of human life, sandwiched between the endless nothing before you were born and the boundless stretch of time after your death.

33. IT ALL EQUALS OUT

Look around. What you're seeing will soon be dead and gone. And soon after, so will everyone else who's watching it too.

Then there'll be no difference between an ancient grandparent and a babe that died in the cradle.

34. LOOK INTO MY EYES

Take time to examine the instincts that guide others.

What are they working towards?

Why do they value and love what they do?

Look at them with a calculating eye, as if their souls were laid open before you. They think their thoughts and opinions should affect you?

Whatever.

35. IT'S NOT SO BAD

Loss is just change. And the universe loves change.

Ever since the Big Bang, things have come into being in the same way and will continue to do so until the end of time. How can you claim then that everything is getting worse? That the world is condemned to turmoil and despair forever?

36. NO EXCEPTIONS

Everything is destined to decay – water, earth, bones, everything. Stone is just compressed shells and sand. Clothing is merely tufts of cotton or the silk from the back end of a worm (if you're fancy). And every breath is the same. In. Out. In. Out.

37. GIVE IT A REST
Enough bitching and grumbling already. Why stress yourself out? Nothing new is happening to get you all riled up.

So what gives?

Is the issue down to what's causing these things? Then take a deeper look.

Is it the results? Then focus on that.

Beyond cause and effect, there's nothing else. Wherever you are in life, look to become a simpler, better person. (The task is the same whether you work at it for one year or one hundred.)

38. REAL HARM?
If someone has done wrong, they've harmed themselves. But what if they haven't done any harm?

39. BAA
Either everything has its roots in some kind of single intelligent source or else it's made up of atoms brought together by chance and evolution.

If it's the former, no part of the whole should complain about its position and purpose.

If it's the latter, again, what are you going to do?

So don't worry. Keep your mind true to yourself. Are you already dead? Are you simply going through the motions? Are you just another sheep in a field, eating grass the same as all the rest?

40. DO THE GODS CARE?
If there are gods (of any religion), they are either powerful or powerless.

If they're powerless, why bother with them?

If they're all-powerful, rather than begging them to be spared this or that problem, why not pray simply to not be disturbed by whatever happens? If they exist and can help at all, surely this is in their power (and won't affect anyone else).

Of course you could say, *'Isn't this something the gods have given me the power to do myself?'* Good point. Then surely you're better off using that power yourself than begging for things outside your control.

Anyway, who says that a god wouldn't give you a helping hand in this way?

So instead of praying to capture the eye of someone you fancy, try praying to avoid lusting after them in the first place.

Or instead of praying to your god to defeat your enemies, pray to be free of your desire to be rid of them.

And instead of praying that you never lose your child, instead pray not to fear the loss of them.

Give this a go and see what happens.

41. FEELING ILL

Epicurus was a smart man. When he was sick, he never spoke about his aches and pains. Instead, he carried on focusing on how the mind could stay distant from the pain even while being a part of the rest of the body. How it was still free to do its own thing. Neither did he give his doctors the chance to boast about their achievements in making him well. He just got on with life, calmly and happily.

So if you're ill, be like Epicurus. Don't let it affect your mind or get caught up in all the nonsense you'll hear or read on Doctor Google (pretty much every expert agrees on this).

Keep doing your thing with the tools at your disposal.

42. HELPING HANDS

When someone is a dick towards you, ask yourself, '*Will there ever be a world without dicks like these?*'

Of course not, so don't ask for the impossible. These people are just a part of everything else in the world. Keep this in mind whenever you come across any liar, troll or idiot. In doing so, you'll find they don't get to you so much.

And don't forget, you already have the ability to deal with these kinds of things.

If people are rude, be polite.

If they are harsh, be gentle.

If they are loud, be quiet.

Remember, you have the power to show people that they've got it wrong, that they're off the mark.

Besides what harm has this caused you? Nothing they've done can really hurt you unless your mind lets it.

Is it so surprising that a dick behaves dickishly? Shouldn't you blame yourself for not expecting this? You had the mind and the ability to realise this and you didn't. And now you're surprised.

Whenever someone winds you up, turn your thoughts inwards first. The mistake is yours – especially if you put your faith in that kind of person or did something for them expecting a reward other than that of doing something good in the world.

Once you've done a good deed, what more do you want? Isn't it enough simply to have done the right thing?

Anything else is like expecting to reward your eyes for seeing or your ears for hearing. It's just what they do.

It's the same with people. We are made to help each other. It's just what we do.

THE TENTH BOOK

> *'Stop all that bleating on about what a good person should be. Be it.'*

1. WHEN OH WHEN?

I sometimes wonder if I'll ever get it.

Will my mind ever become truly good, sincere, transparent and honest with the world around me?

Will I ever be as loving and kind as I want to be?

Will I give up on wanting more, more, more and just be satisfied with what I've got?

Will I give up on hoping that someone will simply look after me and pander to my needs?

And will I stop trying to prolong my life, wishing for another year, another day, another hour?

When will I finally be happy with things how they are and understand that this is all just how it is and that that's OK? It's the way of the universe – good, fair and beautiful.

It's the universe that gives us all life and to which we return after death (where our atoms become something else again).

Will I ever deserve to find my place in all this without complaining and moaning about my fate?

2. DO WHAT YOU DO
Look inside. Pay attention to what your true self is telling you to do.

Do it.

Be OK with this (as long as it'll do you no physical harm of course).

But also listen to your body. Do what it needs (as long as it won't harm your mind or those around you).

Follow these rules without worrying about all the other stuff.

3. CARRY ON CARRYING ON
Whatever happens, you're either ready or you're not.

If it's something crappy that you can cope with, don't resent it, just use what you have to get through to the other side. If it goes beyond what you're capable of, still refuse to resent it – don't let it win.

And don't forget, you can endure anything your mind has decided is endurable by simply viewing the act of endurance as being good for you.

4. WHO'S TO BLAME?
If someone gets something wrong, take time to gently show them their mistake and how they can correct it.

If you don't manage to persuade them, you have two choices – either blame yourself or blame no one.

5. MEANT TO BE?
Whatever happens is just the end of a series of causes and effects that go back to the beginning of time. Your small thread in this tapestry was always going to lead to this moment.

6. A PART OF THE WHOLE
Regardless whether the universe is a random jumble of atoms or some kind of ordered system, I know I'm a part of the wider whole and must follow its rules.

As such, I'm related to everything and everyone else around me. As a part of the universe, then, I'm not going to bitch about anything it sends my way since anything that's good for the whole is good for me.

It's like a body, except that, as far as I know, there's nothing outside the universe that can make it do anything that would harm it.

So, I might as well be relaxed about what comes my way. And because I'm related to all the other parts, I'm not about to do anything which will cause them harm – quite the opposite in fact.

If I keep all this in mind, my life will run smoothly – just like it will for anyone who looks out for others and is ready to do what's needed.

7. ARE THESE YOUR ATOMS?
Everything in the universe will ultimately decay and change form.

If this was some kind of essential evil, the universe simply wouldn't work. Everything is decaying all the time and the natural world is not pre-programmed to harm itself – it wouldn't survive if that was the case.

Even if this process is not part of some intricate system and is, instead, purely random, it's nothing to get stressed about. It's not unnatural or some kind of plot against us.

Ultimately, our atoms will be recycled to become other things. You've already gone through these kinds of changes in your life, taking in atoms from food, transforming them into energy, transforming that into muscle, etc.

You weren't born with all these atoms, and even if you've still got some from back then hanging about, it doesn't undermine the general argument.

8. YOU DO YOUR THING
If you talk about yourself as good, humble, truthful, clear-headed, accepting, rational and all the rest of it, make sure you don't contradict this in real life. And if you do stumble, fix it quick.

Remember, being clear-headed is about paying attention to the details, watching what's really going on. And acceptance means rolling with whatever comes your way, not getting bent out of shape about the coulda, woulda, shoulda.

Being rational is about putting the mind above the body and emotions – above ambition, fear and death. Live up to your claims (though without becoming desperate for others to echo those same claims) and you'll become a different person with a different life.

To carry on being torn and harassed by life is just stupid and cowardly. It's like the boxer who staggers out of the ring bloody and bruised, just barely conscious, but who still pleads, *'Just one more fight,'* only to be beaten again the next day.

So jump aboard your little ship of claims, hang on through rough seas and storms if you can. But if you can't, make for some nearby harbour where you can regroup for a bit.

When you're trying to keep your strengths front and centre, it can help to remember how the universe works. Trees do tree things. Dogs do dog things. Bees do bee things. And rational humans should do rational human things.

9. TIME TO STEP UP
Day-in, day-out, all the idiocy, pointless arguments, laziness and brown-nosing will gang up to obliterate your carefully cultivated clear thinking.

So it's down to you to focus on every single thing, every event, every action and do what needs to be done while ensuring your mind remains focused. In doing so, enjoy the confidence that only someone who's in control of the details can hope to attain.

Will you ever manage to achieve the peace of mind that comes from true integrity? A peace of mind that stems from looking deeper, understanding what's inside every creature and where it fits into the greater scheme of things. One that sees what it is, how it's made and who has power over it.

10. CATCH THIS
Cats love catching birds. Some people love fishing. Others love hunting

big game. Still others love ensnaring people.

If you look at them and what they believe, aren't they all just thieves?

11. EVERYTHING CHANGES

Pay attention to the constant change in the universe around you. Teach yourself how and why it happens. There is nothing that's better at expanding your mind. Because once you realise that you might be gone at any moment, you'll worry less about your husk of a body and be able to devote yourself to higher aims: truth, fairness, being at one with the world around you.

You'll stop caring what others think or say about you. Only two things will really matter: justice and being OK with whatever fate has in store. You'll be able to park all the other worries and distractions. Your only ambition will be to live life true to your higher ideals.

12. THE DIRECT ROUTE

When you know what you have to do, there's no need to guess. If the path ahead is clear, go for it and don't turn back.

Of course, if it's all a bit murky, wait awhile. Get some advice. See if the fog clears.

If other things get in your way, approach with caution, do what you can with what you've got. Always err in the direction that seems the fairest to all. Because this is where your destination lies (and it's also the place where most people fail).

13. ARE THEY WORTH IT?
From the moment you get up, ask yourself, *'Does it really matter if others criticise my actions when I know I'm correct?'* Of course not.

People who are so quick to praise you or blame you are just the same in the rest of their lives. Think about all the stuff they do, what they chase after or take from others they attack – not just with their hands but with the highest part of their selves, the part that's the source of fairness, truth, honour and justice.

14. GIVE AND TAKE
To nature – where everything comes from and everything is destined to return – simply say, *'Give me what you will and take what you want.'*

But don't get all 'up yourself' about it. Ask with simple honesty and goodwill.

15. YOU'RE NOT GETTING ANY YOUNGER
When you're getting on and the end is approaching, live your life as if your home was at the top of some rocky mountain.

After all, why does it matter where you live? As long as you see yourself as a part of everything around you. Let others see you as someone living in tune with nature and the wider universe.

If they can't stand the sight, let them get rid of you. It's better to die than live like them.

16. JUST BE IT
Stop all that bleating on about what a good person should be. Be it.

17. YOU ARE VERY, VERY SMALL
Spend time thinking about all eternity. Consider that everything around you is just a speck in the universe and your time here is but the blink of an eye.

18. BORN TO BE DEAD
Pick up a thing, some random object. Focus on how it is already changing, dissolving and decaying. Everything is born to die.

19. GET OVER YOURSELF
Eating, sleeping, fucking, shitting – what are people like?

All those attitudes they throw up. All the face-saving, the look-at-me Instagramming. Just minutes ago they were sucking up to others.

Wait a few more minutes and they'll do it again. What's the point?

20. NOW THAT'S GOOD
Whatever the universe serves up is for the best (and for the best exactly when it happens).

21. YOU LOVE, I LOVE
Nature loves making rain and whatever else needs to exist. To nature I say, 'What you love, so do I.'

Isn't this the real meaning of 'love will find a way'?

22. ON THE MOVE?
You can carry on living here. You can move somewhere else if you like. Or you can die (in which case, don't worry).

There really are no other choices, so relax.

23. TAKE IT WITH YOU
Living how you should will be the same no matter where you are. On top of a mountain. By the sea. Wherever.

Your mind can always be soaking up the sun on a pure, sandy beach (even when your face is in someone's armpit on public transport).

24. IS YOUR MIND WORKING?
What is your reasoning mind?

What are you supposed to do with it right now?

What use are you putting it to?

Is it doing its job?

Are you drifting away from others and failing to make a connection with them?

Is it so focused on your body, your whims and urges that it can't think about anything else?

25. NO TIME TO RUN AWAY

If you go AWOL from the army, you're a deserter.

But think of the law as our platoon. If we break it, we too are deserters.

Ultimately, if you get wound up by anger, envy or fear, you're breaking with something that's a natural outcome of the universe.

It's a natural law (and one you're fleeing from).

26. NO BIG MYSTERY

Some man ejaculates into a woman and leaves. But this starts a chain of events that can create a new life. How amazing.

The same guy throws some food down his throat and it's transformed into energy and emotion.

Drop your phone, and gravity pulls it to the road.

From the outside, these processes seem mysterious. But just because you can't see them with your eyes, the results are still clear.

27. YOU AGAIN?

Think about how everything that's happening around you is just a rerun of the past. Also consider that it's likely to happen again in future.

Think of all the dramas, large and small, you've experienced time and time again (or which are similar to things you've seen in history books).

Think of governments – first this party, then that, then back to the other.

It's just the same show with different actors.

28. OINK
When you see someone bitching and complaining, picture them as a pig about to be butchered, squealing and squealing.

Someone who chooses instead to hide under their duvet moping in silence is no better.

A reasonable person will go with the flow and embrace the world without all the drama. All the rest can do is tag along.

29. IS THAT IT?
Whatever you're doing, stop and ask yourself, *'Is it the thought that I won't be able to do this anymore the reason I fear death?'*

30. MIRROR IMAGES
When someone offends you, consider whether you have similar faults. Do you too love money, fame and pleasure too much?

Once you realise they're only doing what they do because they are driven by these impulses, you'll be less angry. What else could they have done?

Alternatively, if you can, help them see things another way (you'll help yourself too).

31. SMOKE AND DUST AND PATIENCE
When you see one of today's politicians or celebrities, imagine they are

someone similar who's now long dead. Do the same with yourself – think of a great, great grandparent perhaps. Ask, *'Where are they now?'*

The answer is, nowhere (or at best no one really knows). This will help you see all humanity as simply smoke and dust. And you'll realise that once something changes, it's gone for good.

So why get stressed? Why not just live your life as best you can?

Think about all the good you could be doing but aren't because you're so focused on all this other crap. In reality, it's all just a training ground for your mind to teach it the truth about the universe and your place within it.

Be patient. Learn what life has to teach you. It's like getting used to spicy food or getting a fire hot enough to burn even the largest logs. It takes time.

32. BE TRUE OR DON'T BOTHER
Don't let anyone be able to say that you are not honest and fair.

If anyone thinks this, you should be able to say, hand on heart, they're wrong. Because it's down to you. Only you can be honest and fair and good and all the rest of it.

If you can't do this, why go on?

33. THE OBSTACLE COURSE
What's the best you can say or do with what you have? After all, whatever happens, you are free to say or do what you like. There's no excuse.

Let's face it, you'll never stop complaining until it's as natural for you to follow your true self (whether you're in a hole or a hotel) as it is for an alcoholic to like a tipple. In fact, you should get off on every opportunity you get to be who you really are (and the opportunities are endless).

A wheel won't roll by itself. A fire won't ignite without a spark. Water doesn't appear out of nowhere. There are too many things in the way.

But intelligence, the mind, reason, they're different. They can find a way past any obstacle. Just like a wheel rolling down a slope, a fire leaping up a set of curtains or rain falling from a cloud. You need look no further.

If something is going to stop us, it must only affect our bodies. If not, our minds have to conspire to skew our perceptions or give up reason altogether. Then we can be defeated.

It's one of the curious things in nature. When an obstacle affects some inanimate object, it tends to make it worse. But when someone overcomes those obstacles, they become better.

In short, nothing can truly hurt someone if it doesn't damage the wider universe – and that can only happen if it runs counter to the laws of the universe. The things you call bad luck are never counter to the laws of the universe. So they can't, ultimately, hurt you.

34. LEAVES IN THE WIND

When you know the truth, even a simple saying can bring it home. For example, 'What are people but leaves that fall in the wind?'

Your kids are the leaves. The leaves are also the mass of people around you (the ones that shout and sneer and praise and complain). The leaves are also all those that may remember you once you're gone. They grow in spring and are gone by winter, blown away by autumn gales. They're then replaced by new leaves in turn. And so it goes.

Nothing lasts and yet you chase after it all (or run away when it's scary). It's like they'll be here forever. Soon enough your end will come. Soon after, it'll come for those who mourn you too.

35. THE HEALTHY MIND

A healthy eye's job is to see things as they are, not demand that everything should be shades of green. (That would simply demand a trip to the optician.)

It's the same with hearing and smell. They should tell you about what's happening.

A healthy stomach should digest your food.

And a healthy mind should be ready for whatever comes its way.

A mind that cries, *'Keep my kids from dying'* or *'Make everyone love me'* is like an eye that only wants to see green or a nose that only wants to smell roses.

36. SLIP SLIDING AWAY

No one is so lucky that they can lay on their deathbed without people looking forward to their imminent demise.

These people might say you're clever, good or wise. But some will also mutter under their breath that they're happy to see the back of you, that they always thought you were silently judging them.

Just think of all the reasons you've given others to be glad you're gone.

But as you approach the end of your life, it can be useful to stop and consider that even your friends and family, who you've loved and who've loved you, may well see your passing as a kind of relief.

So why strive to live that little bit longer?

Importantly, don't hold this against them, think well of them, be kind. Don't view death as something that'll tear you away from them but rather die peacefully, slip away. Nature brought you all together and now, nature is untying the knot.

I'm leaving my family and friends. It's not that I'm being dragged off against my will. There's no need to resist, it's just another act of nature.

37. ASK YOURSELF
Whenever you see someone do something, ask *'What's their purpose?'* But first, ask yourself the same question.

38. SO MUCH FOR THE FLESH
Don't forget, it's your inner thoughts that make you do what you do. This is your core self.

Don't get confused between this and the body, that fleshy shell that stops your organs spilling on the street.

The body is just a tool. Without the mind to make everything happen as it should, it's no more use than a writer's keyboard, a baker's spatula or a taxi driver's satnav.

THE ELEVENTH BOOK

> *While other people may try to stop you following the paths of reason and doing the right thing, you don't have to let them succeed. Nor do you have to allow them to prevent you acting towards them with generosity and kindness.'*

1. WHAT DOES IT ALL MEAN?
What does it mean to be a rational human?

Well, it means being able to look within yourself. It means being able to change and develop to be the best version of you. It means enjoying the results of having the most evolved mind in the animal kingdom. It means focusing on the right things no matter what stage of life you're at.

It's not like a TV series which, if suddenly cut short, leaves everything up in the air. Your inner self should have done everything it needs to so that, if your personal show is cut short, you leave nothing unfinished.

A rational person can look at things from the perspective of the wider universe. They can project forward into eternity and understand that everything is part of a larger, cosmic cycle of life, death and change.

They understand that, at a fundamental level, we'll see nothing our parents haven't seen before us. Likewise, our kids won't see anything truly new. It doesn't matter whether you live to just 40 – if you've paid attention to what matters, you'll have seen everything you'll ever need to see. Because it's all the same.

Finally, a rational person will love their fellow humans. They'll value truth and modesty. Above everything else, they'll have self-respect. And because of all this, they'll value justice and fairness.

2. HOW ENCHANTING

It's easy to get swept away with others' performances, whether it's singing, acting, political speeches or the perfect tweet. But you don't have to be.

Break each down to its separate elements – the lyrics, the tune, the individual carefully chosen words. Ask yourself, *'Is this influencing me?'*

It might be embarrassing if the answer is yes. Are you so easily swayed?

Do this for everything you see and hear. Split everything up into its component parts and you'll find it's easier to disengage your emotions and re-engage your reason.

3. READY OR NOT?

It's a wonderful thing to be ready at the hour of your death for whatever it brings – whether that's pure nothingness, the dispersal of your atoms, even an afterlife of some sort.

But this readiness must be the result of an active decision. It can't just be because you want to stick your tongue out at the forces of conformity.

It should be because you've thought about it, deliberated and resisted the urge to descend into petty dramatics.

4. UNSELFISH REWARDS
Have I acted unselfishly? If so, I already have my reward. Keep this thought front and centre and you'll stay the path.

5. YOUR JOB
Ah, that opening dinner party question, *'What do you do?'*

The real answer is: Be good.

But how can you do this if you haven't truly understood how the universe and the people around you really work?

6. IT'S A TRAGEDY
The origin of drama was tragedy – a way of showing all the ups and downs of life (particularly the downs). It was a reminder that shit happens all the time.

We still enjoy this kind of thing on TV today. And since we can enjoy it on the screen, why should we freak out when it happens in real life?

After all, these performances show that people can endure almost anything – despite being driven to outbursts of the *'For fuck's sake!'* variety.

They also give us some useful quotes:

'Sometimes, it's just easier to abide than it is to struggle.' The Dude in *The Big Lebowski*.

'Get busy living or get busy dying.' Andy Dufresne in *The Shawshank Redemption*.

'The things you own end up owning you.' Tyler Durden in *Fight Club*.

And there's a bunch more if you look for them.

Following on from tragedy came comedy (in the original sense). This gave us a good telling off for our vanity, sparing no blushes.

Later, of course, this all degenerated into clever lines and exaggeration. But you have to ask, what's the point of this?

7. DEAL WITH IT
It's pretty obvious that nothing will better prepare you for putting all this thinking into practice than the situation you find yourself in right now.

8. TREES AND PEOPLE
Cut a branch off another branch and it will, of course, become separated from the tree.

It's the same with people. Someone cut off from everyone else is separated from the rest of humanity.

But while the branch isn't responsible for its separation, people often are. They let hate, fear, greed and suchlike divide them from other individuals (all without realising they are cutting themselves off from wider society in the process).

The good news is that it's possible to become reattached.

But if you are continually detaching and reattaching it can become increasingly difficult to ever truly become one again. It's like the difference between a branch that's always been on the tree and one that's grafted on later. Sure, it may be the same tree, but the connection is never quite the same.

9. FAILURE IS FAILURE

While other people may try to stop you from following the path of reason and doing the right thing, you don't have to let them succeed. Nor do you have to allow them to prevent you from acting towards them with generosity and kindness.

You have to protect against both of these, countering them with both resolve and kindness. It would be just as frustrating to fail on either count.

If that happens, it's still a failure of living up to your ideals no matter how you look at it. One stems from a lack of courage, the other from a lack of human empathy.

10. NATURAL JUSTICE

Nature will always be superior to art because all art stems from nature (however abstracted).

It stands to reason that just as art uses all manner of techniques in service of a higher vision, nature does too. Nature gives us justice, and from justice come all manner of other virtues (kindness, generosity, truth).

But it's still about the overarching vision. Justice won't be served if we get hung up on things that are simply distractions or if we're misled into making the wrong decisions.

11. DON'T MOVE

You can get all stressed out chasing your dreams or trying to avoid the crap you think is heading your way.

But in reality, none of this is coming in your direction. You have to go to it.

If you only learn to stop lusting after the one or being afraid of the other, they'll stay exactly where they are.

12. JUST CHILL

Your true, inner self will remain perfectly untroubled as long as it's neither grasping for something it thinks it needs or collapsing and shrinking in fear.

Instead, it'll show its true colours, shining with the honesty and truth inside.

13. STICKS? STONES?

Is someone making fun of me? Well, that's up to them. All I can do is ensure I don't deserve it.

Maybe someone hates me. Again, that's their problem. I'll try to be friendly and helpful to others no matter who they are.

I'll try to show those who hate me that they've got it wrong, but I won't do so in some kind of passive-aggressive manner or by making a big show of it.

This is an attitude that has to come from within – there's no good to be had from holding a grudge and basking in self-pity. After all, what harm can really come from doing the right thing in the moment for the benefit of the world around you?

14. HATING WHAT YOU LOVE
You see people both hate others and also desperately want to be just like them. These people spend so much time planning to one-up others but, at the same time, cower in fear.

15. TRUST ME
Alarm bells should start ringing as soon as someone says, *'I'm going to be honest with you.'*

What are they playing at?

If it's real honesty, it needs no setup. It should be plain to see and hear. It should shine from their eyes (just as you immediately know a lover's meaning when they give you *that* look).

Sincerity and goodness should be so obvious that you can smell them in the air. They should be instantly recognisable.

Fake sincerity is a hidden gun. It's like Red Riding Hood faced with the wolf's false friendship – something to be avoided at all costs. The real deal is so obvious, no one can mistake it for anything else.

16. PERFECTLY INDIFFERENT
Anyone can live a perfectly good life if they are indifferent to things which are fundamentally indifferent to them.

This means first looking at the elements that make up whatever you're faced with before looking at the thing itself.

You have to remember, nothing in the thing itself (object, person, whatever) is ultimately responsible for the opinions we hold about it – that's down to us. We make these judgements and etch them into our brains.

We do this even though we're perfectly capable of refusing (or of hitting the delete button if such opinions creep up on us). It's just mental discipline.

Don't forget, we live short little lives. There's no time to waste on getting annoyed when things aren't how you'd like them to be.

As long as they are part of the natural way of things, don't fret. And if that's not the case, look to yourself and your own values. Head in this direction without caring what others think. There's no blame here.

17. POLYMORPH FOR BEGINNERS
Whatever you encounter, ask: What's it made of? How is it changing? What will it turn into? And then realise, it'll be no worse for the change.

18. NINE RULES FOR AVOIDING OFFENCE
When someone pisses you off, here are some things that could help.

First, remember that we're all part of one big human family. Strip it back further and we're all made of the same atoms (mostly oxygen, carbon, hydrogen, nitrogen, calcium and phosphorus). We're all intelligent, thinking creatures who have scraped our way to the top of the pyramid on this beautiful planet we call home.

Second, think about what the offending person is really like in all the roles they play in their lives. What's pressuring them to think and act the way they do? How much is it all to do with their own self-esteem?

Third, what if they're right? Then you have no reason to complain. And if they're wrong, they've simply made a mistake. Just as no one wants to be lied to, no one wants to do wrong either. Imagine how they'd react if they were accused of being unfair or greedy or stupid. They'd be pretty quick to get angry.

Fourth, look, just between us, you know that you sometimes piss people off too. So really, you're no different than them. On a good day, you're on top of this but the inclination is still there, lurking in a corner of your brain. Chances are, the only thing holding you back is a worry of what others would think.

Fifth, you don't really know for sure they're doing anything wrong. You can't see into their heart. People's motives are never 20:20 (even to themselves). You need to be super clear on this before condemning someone else's behaviour.

Sixth, if you're getting impatient and frustrated by it all, remind yourself, life's short. And when you're dead, who'll really care?

Seventh, it's not what they've done that's getting to you, it's just your opinions of their actions. Ditch this and the offence will evaporate before your eyes. How do you do this? Remind yourself that their offence hasn't done any real harm to you, not to the core of who you are.

Eighth, getting so wound up about it will only really damage you and won't affect the root cause of your offence.

Ninth, last one, it's difficult for anyone to resist genuine kindness. Even when someone is trying to be a total dick, it won't work if you meet it with gentle good humour. Sure, try to correct them if you can or else jump in before they get started with a *'You know, we're both fellow humans in this crazy world. You might want to hurt me but that's not how I roll. You're just going to get all worked up for nothing.'*

Be polite about it. Point out how other animals don't act like this (and they aren't as smart as your accuser). But don't be sarcastic or picky. Be genuinely nice. You're not their school teacher and needn't play to the crowd (whether they're with you in person or hovering over the retweet button). And even if there are others around, treat the situation as if it was just the two of you there alone.

Keep all this in mind and live up to your best self. But even though you're protecting yourself from attack, don't go sucking up to anyone, especially the person offending you. That won't help.

Remember, losing your temper is never the solution. There is more to be gained from being authentically rational and humane, from gentleness and calm. That's strength. Anger is simply weakness.

One more thing, a bonus if you like: haters gonna hate. To expect bad people never to do bad things is just foolish. It's not going to happen. In the same way, tolerating them being dicks to others while getting angry when they do it to you is simply irrational.

19. FOUR THINGS
There are four things your mind will say that'll throw you off track:

1. This thought isn't necessary.
2. This will make people upset.
3. This isn't what I really think (then where did the thought come from?).
4. This will damage my self-esteem.

They're all signs that something's out of whack at the very core of who you are (or it's being overwhelmed by your baser, more insecure instincts).

20. DON'T BE NAUGHTY

All atoms – every single molecule, every element of the Periodic Table – obey the laws of the universe. Some float up into the atmosphere. Some drop like a stone. They don't go trying to rewrite the rules – there'd be no point.

So isn't weird that the one part of you that should know better, your rational mind, is off being naughty somewhere else?

How else could you view its moves towards anger, fear, grief, insecurity and all the rest? The captain of your inner self has gone AWOL.

It's the same whenever your mind throws its toys out of the pram, resenting the way things pan out at any given time. This is how the universe works. It's the way of the world that you've evolved to be a part of. It's been this way forever.

21. WHAT IS GOOD?

If you don't have some overarching aim in life, you'll tend to be all over the place.

But pointing this out isn't enough. We have to be able to say what this aim should be.

It's obvious that it's almost impossible to get the whole of humanity to agree on what we mean by 'good'. The best we can do then is to talk in terms of what improves the lot of humanity as a whole.

If you keep this as your aim, you'll be consistent in your actions throughout your life.

22. CAREFUL WHAT YOU WISH FOR
There's a fable in which an old man is struggling along a road with a pile of sticks on his shoulder. Finally, he decides he can't take this anymore and cries out, *'I'd rather die than carry these sticks a step further.'* Hearing him, Death appears (cloak, scythe, the whole deal) and says, *'How can I help you old man?'* Looking pale, the man quickly replies, *'Please help me get these sticks back on my shoulder.'*

There's a lesson here in being careful what you wish for. Don't trade your peace of mind for excitement, disorder and quick fixes.

23. POPULAR THINKING IS SCARY
The world is crammed full of 'popular' beliefs. We should tell children that these are the real monsters under the bed.

24. IT'S JUST POLITE
If you've got guests coming, say for a barbeque, let them sit in the shade while you sit wherever's left.

25. SMALL FAVOURS?
Back in the day, the philosopher Socrates turned down an invitation from a very famous, very powerful general in Alexander the Great's army.

This invitation would have been seen as a great honour. However, Socrates said he couldn't go because to do so would mean going to his grave with dishonour.

You see, he didn't want to accept something that he'd never be able to repay.

26. INSPIRATION ON YOUR PHONE SCREEN
With all the trials of modern life, it can be difficult to keep your focus on doing the right thing no matter what. It can help to keep a picture of someone who embodies this aspiration close to hand.

27. STARS DON'T LIE
Take time to look up at the stars on a clear night. It's a reminder that there are universal laws that govern everything around you, ones even something as massive and powerful as a star cannot ignore.

28. THIS CHANGES NOTHING
It's like if your best friend plays a joke at the beach, running off with your clothes, leaving you in just your skimpies. At the end of the day, they're still your friend because you love them for so many other things.

29. LEARN THE RULES BEFORE YOU BREAK THEM
Say you want to become a great writer. Before you experiment with

bending the rules, you first have to really understand them. This is even more true in life.

30. ALWAYS A SLAVE
If all you want is to follow others, rational thought is probably not for you.

31. HEARTFELT
'And my heart laughed with me.' (From Homer's *The Odyssey*.)

32. UNDER ATTACK
People always attack and abuse true integrity.

33. TIME FOR EVERYTHING
Just as it's foolish to go looking for summer fruit in winter, it's also unwise to want kids in old age.

34. GRIM NATURE
'*When you kiss your child,*' the philosopher Epictetus said, '*you should remind yourself, they may be dead tomorrow.*'

'*That's terrible, how can you say that?*' we might say to him.

'*Not at all,*' he'd reply, '*it's just an act of nature. Would you think it's terrible that corn ripens in the Summer sun?*'

35. THE NEXT THING
From inedible green grapes to a beautifully ripened bunch of fruit to sweet, tasty raisins – it's just change after change, not into nothing, simply into the next thing.

36. UNBREAKABLE
You can never be robbed of your own free will. No thief can do this.

37. A LESSON
It's important you find a way to keep your impulses under control. They should be focused on the well-being of others and in proportion to what's needed.

Keep a lid on your self-interest.

Don't pay attention to anything you can't directly influence or control (and the only thing you can really control is what goes on in your mind).

38. THE ONLY QUESTION
It's pointless arguing about trivialities. The only question is, will you be rational or not?

39. GOT IT
Which do you want to be, a reasonable person or an unreasonable one?

'*Reasonable,*' you say.

OK, and do you want to be a sick reasonable person or a healthy one?

'Healthy.'

Then why aren't you putting all your efforts into achieving it?

'Because I already have it,' you answer.

Then what is it with all the worry, stress and argument?

THE TWELFTH BOOK

> *'If it's not the right thing to do, don't.*
> *If it's not the truth, keep your mouth shut.'*

1. IN A NUTSHELL

You can have the good life right here, right now. Just stop putting barriers in your own way.

Forget about the past, it's gone. Don't worry about the future, what will be will be. Focus on the now. This minute.

Do the right thing, right now. Be cool with whatever hand nature's dealt you in this present moment (after all, nature has also given you everything you need to deal with it).

Be fair to others. Speak the truth. Act lawfully (as long as the law is just). And ensure your actions are in proportion to what's really happening.

Respect other people's rights but don't let them drag you down or make you forget your values. Don't let your misconceptions distort your actions. And refuse to be ruled by your body's impulses.

As I've said before, some people are dicks. Ignore them.

Time is short. Your time on this planet is brief, so focus on living up to your best self.

Ultimately, you shouldn't fear death, you should fear a life poorly lived. Make the universe proud, become its closest friend, learn its secrets as best you can. And whatever else you do, stand on your own two feet.

2. BE A GOD

When people talk about a god or gods, there's a core idea that these beings can see into your very soul, ignoring all the material stuff around it. In this way, they can focus on what really matters.

Whether gods exist or not, it's a pretty good lesson. If you do the same, you'll stop getting distracted. You'll be able to ignore both designer clothes and cheap rags, mansions and hovels, fame and obscurity – all the costumes and cardboard scenery of modern life.

3. THREE-RING CIRCUS

You're made up of three parts: the body, the breath and the mind.

The first two are yours to look after. The third, however, is truly all yours alone.

Keep everything that may affect the body and breath (but which is not in your control) away from this core thinking part of you – all the miscellaneous stuff that swirls about you, everything others say or do, everything you've done to date, all your worries about the future – and you will be free.

You'll be able to live your life independently of others, in a way that is honest, true and fair.

You see, it's about breaking away from being so attached to stuff that doesn't really matter. It's about refusing to be ruled by time – the past, the future, what's left on the clock. It's about living the life you actually have, the one right in front of you.

That's what will enable you to live the rest of your life without worry, showing kindness to your fellow humans, at peace with the universe.

4. BUT THEY SAID...

Isn't it strange how people these days are so self-absorbed, loving themselves above everyone else, yet are so quick to value others' opinions over their own?

What if some all-powerful being commanded them to immediately tweet every last thing that popped into their heads as soon as it appeared (no matter how embarrassing)? They wouldn't last a day.

Doesn't this prove that we tend to overvalue what others think of us?

5. FORGETFUL GODS?

If there are gods who are perfect in word and deed, who truly love us, can they have really made the mistake of not allowing those who follow their lessons, who are closest of all of us to the divine, to have some kind of afterlife or another go round?

But whatever, if that's the way of it then that's just how it is. It's the natural way of things.

So if there is no afterlife, that's how nature intends it. And if you get all uppity about it, you'll just anger any gods that may exist (and do you really want to go there?).

If the gods are all they're made out to be, would they have really overlooked something like this?

6. PRACTICE MAKES OK
Practice the things you are rubbish at, the things you'll never master.

If you're a righty, for example, your left hand is probably pretty useless at lots of things. But I bet it's rather good at spearing at your food with a fork. It's just a matter of practice.

7. SOUL MUSIC
Consider how you want your body and mind to be when you die. Think about how short life is and the never-ending nothingness that awaits on the other side. And think about how almost everything is so easily broken.

8. IT'S NOT THEM, IT'S YOU
Examine the inner causes of things. Strip away all the external fluff and nonsense. Study the core of pain, pleasure, death and fame. Take a moment to realise how you create your own misery – how problems never come from outside but are born of our own opinions and misperceptions.

9. BOXERS FOR THE WIN
When you're defending your principles, think more like a boxer and less like a sniper. The sniper is forever picking up and putting down their weapon. The boxer is always armed and ready to go.

10. WHAT IS THAT EXACTLY?
Determine what things really are. Split them into what they're made of, what they do and why they exist.

11. IS YOUR PRIVILEGE SHOWING?
Man, we are all so privileged. We all have the power to do the right thing and to accept how the world really is.

12. NO ONE'S FAULT
If you're a religious sort, don't blame the gods for how things are. If gods exist, they can't do anything wrong either on purpose or by accident (or they wouldn't be gods).

Thing is, you can't blame other people either because whatever wrongs they do are always by accident (whether in action or thinking).

Best to just forget blame altogether.

13. TAKE ME TO YOUR LEADER
On this planet, only an idiot or an alien should be surprised by anything that happens in life.

14. STORM'S A-COMING
It's possible we're all doomed by unchanging laws of nature. Or maybe that our prayers and begging are listened to by some kind of higher power. Or maybe it's all just chaos and madness.

If it's the first, why bother resisting?

The second? Well, you can try to follow the rules of whatever holy book takes your fancy and hope for the best.

And if it's chaos? Be thankful that at least you've got your mind to steer you forward. If the chaos overwhelms you, only let it overwhelm your body. No matter what, don't let it wreck your mind.

15. SNUFFED OUT

A candle's flame will shine just as bright until it's extinguished. But will you let the truth, wisdom and justice inside you die before you are finally extinguished?

16. WISHFUL THINKING

As soon as you think somebody's done wrong, ask, *'Am I certain that this is actually wrong?'* And if it is, how do you know that the person responsible isn't already beating themselves up over it?

To wish that other people never do anything wrong is like wishing that too much wine will not lead to a fuzzy head come morning or that babies will never cry or that politicians will always stick to the truth.

Ain't gonna happen.

If they're that sort of person, they're going to do that sort of thing. Either chill out about it or try to do something to fix it.

17. STOP IT BEFORE IT STARTS

If it's not the right thing to do, don't. If it's not the truth, keep your mouth shut.

18. BIG THEN SMALL

Always look at the whole of something. What is it about it that makes such an impression on you? Then break it down into its component parts – its cause, its material make-up, its purpose and how long it's going to last.

19. GET A GRIP

Before it's too late, understand that there is more to you than your kneejerk instincts – something higher, something nobler. Just what is it that's yanking your chain at this moment – fear, jealousy, lust or something else entirely?

20. POINTLESS IS AS POINTLESS DOES

First, don't do anything pointless or random without purpose. Second, make sure that anything you do is in some way good for the world as a whole.

21. MAKING SPACE

Soon enough, you'll be nothing. In fact, pretty soon everything and everyone you see around you will be nothing too. Everything is destined to change and die, it makes room for whatever comes next.

22. ALL OPINIONS

Everything around you is nothing more than the result of your opinions about it – and that opinion comes solely from inside you. Choose to be free of it and it'll be like you've just turned a corner out of a raging storm, everything will be calm.

23. FINISH AT THE FINISH

When you finish any task at the right moment, no harm will come to you or the world around you.

It's the same with life as a whole. It'll stop when it stops, there's no harm to that and it's not wrong to end it when the time is right. But exactly when is governed by nature – nature that's eternally renewing everything in the universe. Whatever serves this purpose is fair.

So it makes sense that the end of a life isn't in any way evil. After all, there's nothing we can do about it. It certainly isn't a source of blame or shame.

Actually, in dying, we're freeing up some atoms to go back into the wider universe, atoms which will become part of something else. So, in some ways, part of us does go on.

24. THREE THINGS

There are three things you should keep in mind.

The first is that you should never act randomly, without purpose or unfairly. Remember, everything that happens is either down to chance or is in some way part of a long string of cause and effect. There's nothing you can do about chance and it's not like you can sue fate for damages.

The second is to consider what's at the core of every creature, from the moment it's born to the second it dies. What's it made of? What will it dissolve into?

And the third is to imagine you are on the International Space Station looking down on Earth. From this perspective, the whole of people's ambitions, worries, joys and despairs would all seem pretty trivial. It wouldn't matter how many times you looked down, you'd basically see the same things, each lasting mere moments. And to think, these are the source of all our pride.

25. EVERYONE HAS ONE
Ditch your opinions and you'll be free. Who's stopping you?

26. AN ANTIDOTE TO ANGER
Whenever you lose it, you're forgetting that everything is subject to the laws of the universe. Others' bad behaviour is none of your business. It will happen over and over no matter what you do. Always has. Always will.

You're also forgetting that what really binds all us clever apes together is not blood and family but our shared intelligence. It's as close to the divine as we get.

Ultimately, nothing really belongs to you. Not your children. Not your body. Not your inner self. Everything comes from the mind.

More than this, everything depends on your opinions and preconceptions. And in the final analysis, the present moment, this right now, is all you have to live or lose.

27. LIVE FAST, DIE POINTLESSLY
Think about those who've lived without limits – those that have done it all: scaled the peaks of fame, plumbed the depths of disaster, surfed the waves of chance.

Where are they now? Smoke, dust, stories.

The examples are legion. Drugged-out actors. Burnt-out executives. Aged rockers chasing one more fix. How pointless are the things people like these chase after.

Surely it's better to focus on being fair and just, showing self-control, doing the right thing. And doing it all with simplicity and humbleness – because those who are so *'Look at me, look how good I am'* are the worst of all.

28. BELIEVE YOUR EYES?

To those who ask, *'Where have you seen this interconnectedness of the universe that you go on about?'* My answer is, *'I see it about me all the time and anyway, I've never laid eyes on my inner self, but I know it's there and I respect it all the same.'*

The power of all manner of unseen forces is at work around us all the time, to me this is obvious and something to be valued.

29. AVOID THE CRACKS

To lead a life full of inner peace, look carefully at everyone around you.

Focus on their core essence, what makes them truly them. What's in their heart? What are they made of? What's their purpose?

Put everything into this. See things for what they are. Give your heart and soul to doing what's fair, speaking the truth and piling one good deed on top of another, over and over – until you can't see the join between them.

30. DIVIDING AND MULTIPLYING

Sunlight is one, singular thing – even when broken up by walls or mountains or any other barrier.

Humanity is one thing too – even when split across a multitude of individual bodies, each with their own, unique qualities.

The mind is also one thing – despite the fact that it can be divided by thoughts.

All the other bits of our bodies are largely indifferent to each other, just cells held together by skin and gravity. But the mind loves the company of other minds, it's the ultimate attraction that connects all people.

31. CUT TO THE CHASE

Why do you want to live so long? Are you craving more sensations? Do you want more stuff? Maybe you want to get bigger muscles or a thinner waist? Or do you want more time to talk and think?

Are any of these things really worth hankering after so much?

If you decide that they're not worth bothering with, then simply focus on pursuing reason and fairness. But if this is, indeed, the case, you have to remember that it'll all go belly up if you carry on chasing all these other things.

32. TINY, TINY, TINY

What a tiny part of eternity each of us gets. Just an instant. A speck of time.

And how little of the world we take up with our bodies or see as we go from place to place.

As you think about this, decide that nothing else is important but to do right by your best self and to deal faithfully with whatever comes your way.

33. ON THE RIGHT TRACK

How are my guiding principles doing? Are they up to the job? Because everything depends on this. Anything else, whether I control it or not, is just dust and ash.

34. CONTEMPTUOUS DEATH

Nothing will enable you to hold death in contempt quite as much as thinking that even those people who consider pleasure good and pain evil still despise it.

35. CARE LESS

When you decide that whatever is happening right now is all fine and good, when you're not bothered whether you've got lots to do or not very much (as long as it's all in harmony with reason), then you won't care whether your time left on this planet is long or short.

36. THIS IS THE END

My friend, you have been a citizen of humanity. Whether this has been for five years or fifty, what does it matter?

Whatever is fair for humanity is fair for one and all. So why complain?

You're not going to be kicked out of humanity by some cruel dictator. When it happens, it'll be entirely natural. It's like the actor who's show is cancelled after a single season by the people who commissioned it in the first place.

That's just the way of things. You're just a one-season sort of person.

The decision, ultimately, is not in your hands. So move on with grace in your heart and a smile on your face.

AND NOW THE CREDITS
(OTHERWISE KNOWN AS BOOK 1)

> *I would just like to thank the Academy for this wonderful award (though as a Stoic, I'm not too bothered either way). However, as I'm here, I want to take a few minutes to mention some people who've had a massive impact on my life...*

My grandfather Verus taught me to be gentle and not easily angered.

My dad gave me my sense of modesty and manliness.

My mum taught me to be generous and live a simple life. She helped me resist intending any evil to those around me. Thanks Mum.

My great-grandfather gave me my love of learning.

My teacher, among other things, taught me to love hard work, not to go chasing after every fancy that entered my head and to keep my nose out of others' business.

Diognetus taught me not to get caught up in the trivialities of everyday life. He helped me view the world through sceptical eyes, not easily believing what I see or gambling my future on games of chance. He taught me to not be easily offended by what others say. And he's the one who turned me on to philosophy.

Rusticus helped me get over myself. He showed me that I didn't have it all figured out (even when I thought I did) and stopped me from looking like an idiot with every word that came out of my mouth. He helped me speak and write plainly and simply – and to make sure I really understood the facts in detail (not just whatever a thirty-second news bulletin managed to squeeze in). He advised me not to jump on every new fashion or blow my money on flashy outfits. He taught me to be quick to accept an apology and move on. And he introduced me to the work of the philosopher Epictetus, who left a powerful legacy on my life.

Apollonius taught me to take action, not to leave things to chance and never to give up my sense of reason. This gave me an unflappable composure (no matter how tough things got). He brought together both an unassuming character and a passion for what mattered. And he helped me accept the help and gifts of my friends without either feeling in their debt or pretending I didn't care.

Sextus taught me generosity. He gave me a superb example of someone who's a great father and who lived a natural life with dignity, who looked out for others and who had enormous patience with fools and chatterboxes. His charm was more powerful than any flattery, and everyone respected him. He was also methodical, able to boil things down to what was important and essential in life and deed. I never saw him get bent out of shape – he was always calm and kind. You knew when he approved without him making it a big thing. And even though he was highly educated, he never made a show of it.

Professor Alexander turned me off from finding faults with everyone and everything. He taught me you shouldn't jump on every little thing others get wrong – from a mispronounced word to a mistimed tweet. It's better to demonstrate the right approach by slipping it into something you say (especially if you do this while agreeing with what they're saying).

Fronto made me realise that anger, underhandedness and deceit rub up closely with absolute power and that those who sit in the upper reaches of society rarely know what's going on with everyone else.

Alexander the Platonist warned me against saying, *'I'm too busy'* too often. He taught me to keep it for when it was really necessary and not shirk my responsibilities to work, society and my family.

Catulus taught me never to shrug it off when a friend was angry with me (even if they were being unreasonable) but to try to get back on good terms. He also encouraged me to speak well of my teachers and to be genuine and loving to my kids.

My brother Severus showed me what it means to love family, truth and justice. He introduced me to the works of some of the great thinkers and to the core ideas of how a community relies on equality and freedom of speech. From this, I learned that a nation exists to support the freedom of its citizens.

He also encouraged my love of philosophy (though tempered by treating every thought critically and rationally). He taught me to help others by default, to remain optimistic and to always be confident in the love of my friends. He was always straight with those who angered him (you knew where you stood with Severus).

My self-control, sense of purpose and good humour in the face of all the problems of modern life, I owe to Maximus. He managed to balance both dignity and charm and always got on with things without fuss or drama. He left people with the impression that he always spoke his mind and did the right thing by his conscience. He was never moody, never pretended to be happy when he wasn't, and he didn't allow anger or jealousy to cloud his thoughts and drive his actions. He never seemed surprised or scared by events. No one could intimidate or embarrass him either. His charity, loyalty and forgiving nature were simply in his DNA. I can't imagine that anyone felt either inferior or superior to Maximus. What's more, he loved a joke.

From my adopted father, the Emperor Antoninus Pius, I learned to stick to the decisions I made. He helped me become compassionate and to ignore praise. I admired his work ethic and the way he stuck at his tasks. He was always willing to listen when it came to anything that was for the good of society. I learned that rewards should be in proportion to merit. He knew when to be strict and when to chill out (also when to keep it in his pants).

Antoninus also understood that his friends had their own lives and didn't try to dominate their time. He gave every question that came to him careful and deliberate thought (and never dismissed anything on his initial gut feel and assumptions). His friendships were long lasting – simple, honest and without show. In everything he did, he considered the details, understood the possible consequences and worked to determine the best solution. And he cared for the empire with careful planning and by avoiding waste.

He wasn't superstitious about gods and he didn't suck up to other people. He knew that it was better to demonstrate self-control and was suspicious of admiring something new just because it was new. What's more, he wasn't bothered whether people looked up to him or not and, while he enjoyed the benefits of being wealthy, he didn't chase wealth for its own sake and was just as happy in modest surroundings.

He didn't shoot his mouth off about this or that. He didn't nitpick everything others said or did. He certainly respected those who were knowledgeable and wanted to learn, though he didn't talk down to those who didn't.

From him, I learned to take care of my body without obsessing over how I look. He taught me to relax, to avoid jealousy and to be quick to recognise others' achievements (whatever they are). And when he did get sick, he'd soon get back to work afterwards (if anything, with more energy and purpose than before).

Antoninus didn't keep many secrets – and most of those he did were to do with matters of state. He wasn't big into grand gestures. He was always more focused on what was necessary to achieve a public good than what would look good in the eyes of others. He didn't sneak off to the baths when people needed him and was content with whatever food he ate or clothes he wore.

One example that sums him up was how he treated a tax collector who targeted him by mistake. He didn't get angry or lose it. It was more his style to weigh up the pros and cons – without either rushing or hesitating. He'd make decisions calmly and consistently but also with certainty and with fairness.

Ultimately, he was equally able to enjoy or deny himself all the stuff and nonsense that makes so many people crazy.

If there are gods, I should thank them for giving me good grandparents and parents, a good sister, good teachers, companions and friends (well, good for the most part anyway). I'm thankful I never fell out with my friends despite being the sort that might well do so if circumstances went a certain way.

I'm also thankful that I didn't have sex too early or feel the need to prove I was a 'real man'.

I had a father who helped me avoid being too arrogant and showed me that I didn't need all the masses of stuff, legions of people or empty luxuries to live a good life. He taught me I could live like pretty much anyone else and still be able to lead my people.

I had a brother, Lucius, who challenged me to maintain my self-discipline and whose affection I found so disarming.

I was also fortunate to have children who were smart and healthy. I was fortunate too to be merely average at things such as rhetoric, poetry and other studies that could have easily consumed all my time if I hadn't found them so tricky. Freed from trying to perfect these things, I could promote my teachers to the positions they deserved without worrying that they were too young or else putting it off and promising them rewards at some later date.

I'm thankful that I met Apollonius, Rusticus and Maximus. They gave me a true picture of how to live a rich inner existence. It meant that I had no excuse for leading anything other than my best life. I may not be there yet, but that's solely down to me.

I feel blessed that my body has stood up to everything I've put it through. I'm glad I never hooked up with Benedicta or Theodotus and feel lucky that I escaped from other infatuations unscathed.

I'm thankful that, though Rusticus and I argued on many occasions, I never did anything so dumb that I'd regret it later. I'm also grateful that I got to spend so much time with my mum in the final years before her early death.

I'm lucky that whenever I found someone in need that I wanted to help, I was never told I couldn't afford it. Fortunately, I was also never in a position to need such help myself.

I am so thankful to have found my wife – someone so loving, kind and unpretentious.

I'm glad I attracted great teachers for my kids.

Finally, I'm grateful that for all my love of philosophy, I didn't end up learning from some hair-splitting pedant or wasting my time reading pointless theory.

For all this, I am truly thankful.

INDEX OF MAIN THEMES

INDEX OF MAIN THEMES

WHEN YOU LOSE IT AND GET ANGRY

Book 2 – meditations 1 & 10
Book 4 – meditations 7, 26 & 28
Book 5 – meditations 25 & 28
Book 6 – meditations 6, 20, 26, 27 & 41
Book 7 – meditations 22, 24, 26 & 65
Book 8 – meditations 4 & 8
Book 9 – meditations 24 & 42
Book 10 – meditations 25 & 30
Book 11 – meditations 13 & 18
Book 12 – meditations 16, 19 & 26

WHEN YOU WANT TO BE AND DO GOOD

Book 4 – meditations 10, 17, 18, 22 & 25
Book 5 – meditation 31
Book 6 – meditations 7, 30 & 45
Book 7 – meditations 15, 44, 52, 53 & 69
Book 8 – meditations 1, 5 & 22
Book 9 – meditations 16 & 31
Book 10 – meditations 1, 8, 16 & 32
Book 11 – meditations 21 & 26
Book 12 – meditations 17 & 29

WHEN YOU WANT TO BE MORE DISCIPLINED

Book 3 – meditation 8
Book 6 – meditation 22
Book 8 – meditation 19
Book 9 – meditation 12
Book 10 – meditation 3

WHEN YOU'RE TEMPTED BY FAME

Book 4 – meditations 16, 19, 33 & 35
Book 6 – meditation 18
Book 7 – meditations 21, 34, 36 & 62
Book 8 – meditations 1, 3, 21 & 25
Book 9 – meditations 27, 29 & 30
Book 10 – meditations 8, 13, 34 & 36
Book 12 – meditation 27

WHEN YOU KNOW YOU NEED TO BE HONEST

Book 4 – meditation 33
Book 10 – meditation 32
Book 11 – meditation 15
Book 12 – meditations 17 & 29

WHEN YOU'RE TEMPTED TO BLAME SOMEONE OR SOMETHING

Book 8 – meditations 14 & 17
Book 9 – meditations 18, 22, 27 & 38
Book 10 – meditations 4, 10, 13, 19, 30 & 37
Book 11 – meditation 18
Book 12 – meditations 12 & 16

WHEN YOU NEED TO HANDLE CONFRONTATION

Book 5 – meditations 22 & 28
Book 6 – meditations 6 & 27
Book 7 – meditation 26
Book 8 – meditation 17
Book 9 – meditations 11 & 42
Book 10 – meditation 4
Book 11 – meditation 18
Book 12 – meditation 16

INDEX OF MAIN THEMES

WHEN YOU'RE STRUGGLING TO DEAL WITH CHANGE
Book 2 – meditation 3
Book 4 – meditations 1, 3, 23, 42, 43, 45, 46 & 49
Book 5 – meditation 23
Book 6 – meditations 15 & 37
Book 7 – meditations 18, 23, 25, 49 & 75
Book 8 – meditations 6 & 20
Book 9 – meditations 17, 21 & 35
Book 10 – meditations 7, 11 & 27

WHEN YOU'RE WORRIED BY THE PROSPECT OF DYING
Book 2 – meditations 2, 11, 12 & 12½
Book 3 – meditation 14
Book 4 – meditations 5, 37, 47, 48 & 50
Book 6 – meditations 2, 24, 28 & 56
Book 7 – meditations 6, 18, 23, 32, 35, 40, 44, 50, 51 & 56
Book 8 – meditations 25, 31 & 37
Book 9 – meditations 3, 21 & 33
Book 10 – meditations 29 & 36
Book 11 – meditations 3 & 34
Book 12 – meditations 7, 15, 23, 34, 35 & 36

WHEN YOU WANT TO BE BETTER AT SERVING OTHERS
Book 3 – meditation 4
Book 4 – meditations 12 & 37
Book 5 – meditations 6 & 22
Book 6 – meditations 7, 45 & 54
Book 7 – meditations 5, 13, 31, 36, 73 & 74
Book 8 – meditation 23
Book 9 – meditations 9, 11 & 31
Book 11 – meditation 21
Book 12 – meditation 20

WHEN YOU WANT TO DO WITHOUT STUFF

Book 2 – meditation 5
Book 3 – meditation 16
Book 4 – meditation 24
Book 5 – meditations 6 & 15
Book 6 – meditation 30
Book 7 – meditations 27, 31 & 52
Book 8 – meditation 1
Book 9 – meditations 2 & 29
Book 11 – meditations 22 & 28
Book 12 – meditations 2 & 27

WHEN YOU WANT TO GLIMPSE THE BIGGER UNIVERSAL PICTURE

Book 4 – meditation 45
Book 5 – meditation 8
Book 6 – meditations 1, 36, 38 & 46
Book 7 – meditations 9, 48 & 75
Book 9 – meditations 1, 9, 11, 28, 29 & 35
Book 10 – meditations 5 & 26

WHEN IT DOESN'T SEEM THAT FATE IS ON YOUR SIDE

Book 3 – meditations 3 & 16
Book 4 – meditations 33 & 34
Book 5 – meditations 8 & 10
Book 6 – meditation 44
Book 7 – meditations 46 & 57
Book 8 – meditations 15 & 23
Book 10 – meditations 1, 6, 11 & 28
Book 11 – meditations 11 & 20
Book 12 – meditations 1, 32, 35 & 36

INDEX OF MAIN THEMES

WHEN YOU'RE FEELING LUCKY (OR DOOMED)
Book 2 – meditation 3
Book 6 – meditations 10, 36 & 44
Book 7 – meditations 41 & 75
Book 8 – meditations 6, 7 & 23
Book 9 – meditations 1 & 35
Book 11 – meditation 6
Book 12 – meditations 14 & 24

WHEN YOU NEED TO FOCUS
Book 2 – meditation 14
Book 3 – meditation 4
Book 4 – meditations 24 & 32
Book 6 – meditation 32
Book 7 – meditations 29 & 30
Book 8 – meditations 5, 22 & 44

WHEN YOU WANT TO CRY FREEDOM AND DO YOUR OWN THING
Book 3 – meditations 6, 9, 11 & 12
Book 4 – meditations 3 & 46
Book 5 – meditations 10, 11, 19, 20, 29 & 34
Book 6 – meditations 8, 16, 42 & 51
Book 7 – meditations 2, 12, 14, 16, 20, 45, 54, 55, 67 & 68
Book 8 – meditations 3, 16, 28, 29, 32, 41, 47 & 48
Book 10 – meditations 3, 23, 24, 32 & 33
Book 11 – meditations 1, 9, 16, 18, 30 & 36
Book 12 – meditations 3, 8, 14 & 19

WHEN YOU JUST NEED TO HANG IN THERE

Book 2 – meditation 17

Book 4 – meditations 2, 7, 8 & 49

Book 5 – meditations 1, 9, 18, 20 & 25

Book 6 – meditations 2, 10, 11, 19, 22, 29, 30 & 33

Book 7 – meditations 33, 38, 51, 61, 64 & 70

Book 8 – meditations 12, 28, 36 & 46

Book 9 – meditation 41

Book 10 – meditations 3 & 31

WHEN YOU'RE TAKING THINGS TOO MUCH TO HEART

Book 2 – meditations 7 & 11

Book 3 – meditations 6 & 7

Book 4 – meditations 8 & 44

Book 5 – meditations 26, 35 & 36

Book 6 – meditations 32, 41 & 52

Book 7 – meditations 14, 31, 38, 43, 64 & 71

Book 8 – meditations 4 & 7

Book 9 – meditations 1, 31, 40 & 42

Book 10 – meditation 25

Book 11 – meditations 16 & 37

WHEN YOU WANT TO LIVE IN THE HERE AND NOW

Book 2 – meditation 14

Book 3 – meditation 10

Book 4 – meditation 48

Book 7 – meditations 8 & 69

Book 8 – meditations 5, 22, 36 & 44

Book 9 – meditation 29

Book 11 – meditation 7

Book 12 – meditation 26

INDEX OF MAIN THEMES

WHEN YOU NEED TO KEEP IT TOGETHER

Book 7 – meditation 58
Book 8 – meditations 39 & 41
Book 9 – meditations 7, 26 & 42
Book 10 – meditation 31
Book 11 – meditation 19
Book 12 – meditation 19

WHEN YOU NEED TO MAKE THE RIGHT CALL

Book 3 – meditations 6, 9, 11, 13 & 15
Book 4 – meditations 11, 22 & 38
Book 5 – meditations 10, 11, 12, 19, 34 & 35
Book 6 – meditations 3, 8, 13, 17, 52 & 57
Book 7 – meditations 2, 4, 17, 44, 55, 68 & 72
Book 8 – meditations 7, 11, 13, 14, 28, 29, 38 & 49
Book 9 – meditations 7, 15, 18, 22, 25 & 34
Book 10 – meditations 18, 26 & 37
Book 11 – meditations 2, 10, 16, 17, 19, 23 & 37
Book 12 – meditations 8 & 18

WHEN YOU'RE DROWNING IN SELF-PITY

Book 4 – meditation 7
Book 5 – meditation 8
Book 7 – meditations 14, 58 & 70
Book 8 – meditations 9 & 18
Book 9 – meditation 41
Book 10 – meditations 3 & 28

WHEN YOU WANT TO CONNECT WITH YOUR FELLOW HUMANS
Book 2 – meditation 1
Book 4 – meditations 4, 6, 26 & 29
Book 5 – meditations 20, 22, 28, 30,
Book 6 – meditations 12, 20, 27, 39, 50 & 53
Book 7 – meditations 13, 26, 30, 62 & 71
Book 8 – meditations 12, 17 & 34
Book 9 – meditations 3, 9, 11, 20, 22, 27 & 42
Book 10 – meditations 6, 30 & 36
Book 11 – meditations 1, 8, 13, 18 & 24
Book 12 – meditations 16, 20 & 30

WHEN YOU NEED TO RE-ENGAGE YOUR REASON AND RATIONALITY
Book 3 – meditations 9 & 11
Book 4 – meditations 12, 13, 16 & 30
Book 5 – meditations 14 & 32
Book 6 – meditations 14, 23, 26 & 30
Book 7 – meditations 17, 24, 53, 55 & 75
Book 8 – meditations 40 & 41
Book 9 – meditations 8, 10, 26 & 39
Book 10 – meditation 12
Book 12 – meditations 1 & 14

WHEN YOU NEED TO SEE REALITY FOR WHAT IT REALLY IS
Book 3 – meditation 11
Book 6 – meditation 31
Book 7 – meditations 15, 24 & 29
Book 9 – meditations 15, 25, 36 & 37
Book 10 – meditations 9, 18 & 35
Book 11 – meditations 2, 17 & 23
Book 12 – meditations 2, 8, 10, 18 & 29

INDEX OF MAIN THEMES

WHEN YOU KNOW YOU NEED TO TAKE ACTION

Book 2 – meditations 4 & 13
Book 6 – meditations 42, 50 & 51
Book 7 – meditations 12 & 55
Book 8 – meditation 2
Book 9 – meditations 5, 16 & 29
Book 10 – meditations 12 & 13

WHEN YOUR OPINIONS ARE GETTING IN THE WAY OF REALITY

Book 2 – meditations 13 & 15
Book 4 – meditations 3, 11 & 39
Book 6 – meditations 8 & 52
Book 7 – meditations 2, 16 & 68
Book 8 – meditations 28 & 47
Book 9 – meditations 13, 15 & 42
Book 10 – meditation 3
Book 11 – meditations 16 & 18
Book 12 – meditations 8, 22, 25 & 26

WHEN THE SHIT HITS THE FAN

Book 2 – meditation 1
Book 4 – meditations 6, 7, 8 & 49
Book 5 – meditations 18 & 20
Book 6 – meditations 11, 50 & 58
Book 7 – meditations 22 & 61
Book 8 – meditations 32, 33, 35, 46 & 50
Book 9 – meditations 27 & 41
Book 10 – meditations 19, 31, 33 & 35
Book 12 – meditation 22

Made in the USA
Middletown, DE
02 July 2020